"At last! A comprehensive time-management book that's exciting to read. If you only have time to read one book this year, this is it!"
—Steven Ford, Director, Marketing Communications, Texas Instruments

Revolutionize the way you manage time with this easy-to-use program for increasing your personal productivity without working harder or longer. It shows exactly how to focus on high-payoff activities and eliminate time-wasting behavior and procrastination. Drawing on the work of thousands of men and women in seminars across the country, the message of this extraordinary guide goes straight to the heart of the time-management challenges most of us face, providing invaluable techniques on how to:

- Recognize and overcome your hidden hang-ups about time
- Set the right goals for short-term *and* long-term success
- Delegate so that teamwork is most effective
- Have the shortest, most productive meetings
- Create the ideal working environment for both high-level productivity and your own comfort
- Cope when your sense of priorities clashes with others'
- Handle unexpected job emergencies

LESSON #1: Don't procrastinate. Spend time with this book today—and you'll be saving a lot of time tomorrow!

"Good, practical, understandable time-management ideas in an easy-to-use format."
—Charles Cook, President, American Universal Insurance Group

"Peter Turla's approach to time management is both enjoyable and practical. His time-saving ideas have received rave reviews from our people."
—Jeri Drefs, Vice-President, Treasurer, *Newsweek*

"A few hours reading *Time Management Made Easy* has given me hundreds of hours' return on my investment."
—John Renesch, Director, Sterling and Stone, Inc.

ABOUT THE AUTHORS

Peter Turla is one of the world's leading authorities on improving productivity and effectiveness, and has appeared on more than 200 radio and television shows. His exciting and innovative ideas have been featured in dozens of publications, including *Industry Week*, the *Los Angeles Times*, the *Korean World Executive*, the *London World News*, and *USA Today*. Because of his entertaining and informative style of presenting time-management concepts and strategies, he is in great demand as a speaker. Many of his clients have found his ideas so significant, they've invited him back several times a year for the last 15 years. One of his clients, a Malcolm Baldridge National Quality Award winner, had him return for six encore presentations in a single year.

Kathleen L. Hawkins, vice-president of the National Management Institute, has been a reading, writing, and management consultant for 15 years. Thousands of people from all levels of business, government, and industry have taken her courses. Ms. Hawkins is co-author with Peter Turla of *Time Management Made Easy* and of the bestselling audio-cassette *How to Organize Yourself to Win*. She wrote a column for *Success* magazine for five years, and has had four books and more than 200 articles published nationally and internationally on how to increase personal and professional effectiveness.

TIME

MANAGEMENT

MADE EASY

Peter Turla

TIME

MANAGEMENT

MADE EASY

Peter A. Turla

President
National Management Institute

With

Kathleen L. Hawkins, M.A.

Vice President
National Management Institute

Drawings by David Flores

A PLUME BOOK

PLUME

Published by the Penguin Group

Penguin Books USA Inc., 375 Hudson Street, New York, New York 10014, U.S.A.

Penguin Books Ltd, 27 Wrights Lane, London W8 5TZ, England

Penguin Books Australia Ltd, Ringwood, Victoria, Australia

Penguin Books Canada Ltd, 10 Alcorn Avenue, Toronto, Ontario, Canada M4V 3B2

Penguin Books (N.Z.) Ltd, 182–190 Wairau Road, Auckland 10, New Zealand

Penguin Books Ltd, Registered Offices: Harmondsworth, Middlesex, England

Published by Plume, an imprint of Dutton Signet, a division of Penguin Books USA Inc.
Previously published in a Dutton edition.

First Plume Printing, May, 1994

10 9 8 7 6 5 4

Portions of this book have appeared in *Success* magazine.

 REGISTERED TRADEMARK—MARCA REGISTRADA

LIBRARY OF CONGRESS CATALOGING IN PUBLICATION DATA:

Turla, Peter A.

    Time management made easy.

    1. Time management.   I. Hawkins, Kathleen L.

II. Title.

HD38.T88   1983   650.1   83-5690

ISBN: 0-452-27202-5

Printed in the United States of America

To Donald M. Dible

CONTENTS

1

INVESTIGATE YOUR RELATIONSHIP WITH TIME

When you finish this chapter, you will have:

• Revealed your subconscious feelings about time
• Analyzed how wisely you manage your time

Time is highly personal. We all receive exactly the same number of hours in a day, but each of us uses these hours differently. The way we elect to spend our time determines the quality of our lives. Some people always seem to have plenty of time to get their work done and to enjoy life. Many of us, however, often compromise our creativity and our natural sense of things in favor of daily routines. We grudgingly follow imposed schedules while secretly rebelling inside. We struggle with interruptions, paperwork, and procrastination while we yearn for more freedom, more flexibility, and more time. As we go through our lives feeling controlled by clocks, deadlines, and schedules, we may have many mixed feelings about time and how we use it.

REVEAL YOUR SUBCONSCIOUS FEELINGS ABOUT TIME

1. Find a quiet place where you can work undisturbed for ten minutes.
2. On the following list of twenty words, to the right of each word, jot down an abstract symbol that signifies what feelings the word evokes for you. Use lines, circles, spirals, arrows, and the like (see Figure 1). Do not use representational symbols such as a happy face for the word enjoy, a clock for the word time, or a star for the word perfect.
3. If you hesitate on a word, indicate that with a check to the left of the word. Take a moment to think of a symbol. If no ideas come to you, move on.

Begin.

1. BOSS

2. WORK

3. TIME

4. TRIVIA

5. DEADLINES

6. ASSERTIVE

7. INTERRUPTIONS

8. PAPERWORK

9. TELEPHONE

10. WORK ENVIRONMENT

11. FRUSTRATION

12. ORGANIZED

13. MYSELF

14. COMMITMENT

15. PROCRASTINATE

16. ENJOY

17. DISLIKE

18. DECISION

19. DELEGATE

20. PERFECT

When you have completed the *Time Symbols Test,* connect similar symbols with a line. Work with one shape at a time. For example, draw a line between all circular symbols. Figure 1 is a profile of a busy man who is fairly content with his position as a business consultant for a large company. While discussing the circular symbols on his test, he stated that he has an expanded sense of time in which he believes anything is possible. When he procrastinates, however, time becomes boxed in. His symbol for himself reveals expansion, progression, and growth. There is similar motion in his decision-making process, with his final decision being one of clarity and wholeness. Regarding the meaning of his jagged symbols, he admitted to resentment of authority figures and the deadlines they impose. He is much happier working independently and setting his own deadlines.

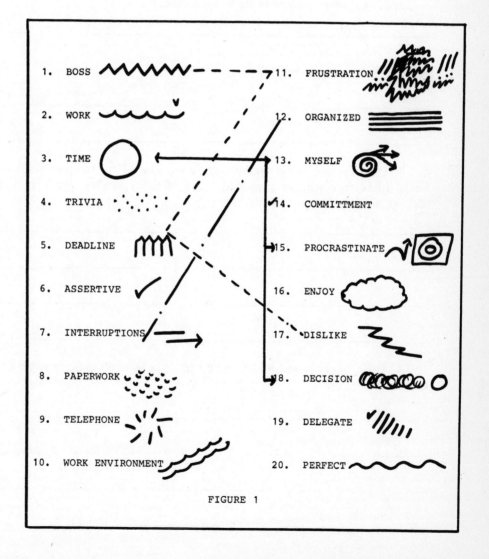

FIGURE 1

Now think through each set of your own symbols. Record your discoveries in the spaces provided.

1. What does each set of symbols represent for you?

_____

_____

_____

_____

2. How do the symbols relate to each other?

_____

_____

_____

3. Does the size of the symbol signify anything? For example, whereas a large circle might represent an expanded sense of time, smaller circles may indicate feelings of limitation or insignificance.

_____

_____

_____

4. Does the pressure with which you drew the symbols indicate stress or intense emotion?

_____

_____

_____

5. Are your lines flowing, jagged, angular, bold, or disconnected? Does this relate in any way to your attitudes about those particular words?

_____

_____

_____

_____

6. Did you hesitate on any of the words because you were unable to think of a symbol for them? Which words?

_____

Does this suggest a block regarding these concepts?

_____

_____

7. What are the patterns of meaning that your Time Symbols Test reveals? Don't try to find significance in every little mark you drew; instead, look for particular trends.

_____

_____

_____

Keep the above insights about yourself in mind as you fill in the following questionnaire to analyze how wisely you manage your time.

How Wisely Do You Manage Your Time?

	OFTEN	SOMETIMES	RARELY
1. Do you write daily to-do lists?	——	——	——
2. Do you prioritize your to-do lists according to which items have the highest payoff for you?	——	——	——
3. Do you finish all the items on your to-do list?	——	——	——
4. Do you update in writing your professional and personal goals?	——	——	——
5. Is your desk clean and organized?	——	——	——
6. Do you put everything in its place?	——	——	——
7. Do you effectively deal with interruptions?	——	——	——
8. Can you easily find items in your files?	——	——	——
9. Are you assertive?	——	——	——
10. Do you allow yourself quiet time during which you can work undisturbed every day?	——	——	——
11. Do you deal effectively with long-winded callers?	——	——	——
12. Do you focus on preventing problems before they arise rather than solving them after they happen?	——	——	——
13. Do you make the best use of your time?	——	——	——
14. Do you meet deadlines with time to spare?	——	——	——
15. Are you on time to work, to meetings, and to events?	——	——	——
16. Do you delegate well?	——	——	——
17. Do subordinates cooperate enthusiastically on projects you assign them?	——	——	——
18. When you are interrupted, can you return to your work without losing momentum?	——	——	——
19. Do you do something every day that moves you closer to your long-range goals?	——	——	——
20. Can you relax during your free time without worrying about work?	——	——	——
21. Do people know the best time to reach you?	——	——	——
22. Do you do your most important work during your peak energy hours?	——	——	——
23. Can others carry on most of your responsibilities if you are absent from work?	——	——	——
24. Do you begin and finish projects on time?	——	——	——
25. Do you handle each piece of paperwork only once?	——	——	——

Your Score

Give yourself 4 points for every *often* you checked. Give yourself 2 points for every *sometimes*. Give yourself 0 points for every *rarely*.

Add your points together and compare yourself with the scale below:

81–100: You manage your time very well. You are in control of most situations.

61–80: You manage your time well some of the time. However, you need to be more consistent with the time-saving strategies you already are using.

41–60: You are slipping. Don't let circumstances get the best of you. Apply the techniques in this book right away.

21–40: You are losing control. You are probably too disorganized to enjoy any quality time. Implement the ideas in this book today!

0–20: You are overwhelmed, scattered, frustrated, and most likely under a lot of stress right now. Immediately put into practice the techniques in this book. Every week review the chapters that deal with your problem areas until you begin to see the light.

Your Action Plan

A. Now that you are more aware of your time-management challenges, make a list of problem areas you want to change.

1. _____

2. _____

3. _____

4. _____

5. _____

B. We can't really manage our time until we learn to manage ourselves. Much bad time management is the result of bad habits we've developed through the years. Read the next chapter now to break those patterns that work against you.

QUOTES TO CONSIDER

"Time is a measure of experience in eternity."

—Ernest Holmes

"Dost thou love life? Then do not squander time; for that's the stuff life is made of."

—Benjamin Franklin

"All my possessions for a moment of time."

—Queen Elizabeth I
(Last words)

2

HOW TO MAKE A HABIT OF GETTING THINGS DONE

When you finish this chapter, you will be able to:

- Discuss the nature of habits
- Break out of self-made ruts
- Expand your comfort zones
- Kick self-defeating habits
- Follow your own personalized habit-control action plan

Resolutions, as we all know, are easy to make—and easy to break. Not so with habits; they're pretty difficult to break without applying a good deal of conscious effort. As you read this book, you will learn enough new techniques to make you an expert on time management. But how can you make what you learn stick? How can you avoid slipping back into all those old, discouraging patterns of mismanaging time? To begin, let's examine the nature of habits themselves.

HABITS—BEHAVIOR WITHOUT THINKING

A habit, as defined by Webster's dictionary is: "A constant, often unconscious inclination to perform some act, acquired through its frequent repetition. A habit is an established trend of the mind or character."

Almost everything we do begins as a constant effort. When we learn something through repetition, we delegate most of the activity to our subconscious minds. This way, our conscious minds are freed to go on to something new. Our lives are composed of thousands of useful habits such as waking up at a certain time in the morning and fulfilling our job responsibilities. Even perception itself is a habit. When we were babies, we learned through trial and error to identify certain shapes, sounds, textures, tastes, and smells; now we automatically and habitually recognize certain sensations without having to consciously think about it.

Unfortunately, habits do not discriminate as to what is good or bad for us. Anything we repeat can become a habit. A daily office routine can become mechanical just because that's the way we've always done it. Likewise, we often develop certain habits toward problem-solving. For example, using only four lines, connect all the dots below without lifting your pencil.

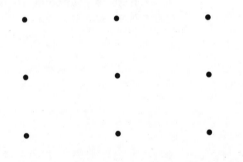

It takes most people about an hour to solve this puzzle because they automatically close the dots into a square in their minds. Then they assume that a line needs a beginning and an ending, so they put a dot at each end. It is not until they break free of established mental sets that they see things differently and can find the solution (see page 16 for answer).

If something as complicated as problem-solving can become a habit, imagine how quickly we can get in the habit of doing mundane chores. We run the risk of letting work pile up just because that's the way we've always done it. Procrastinating and feeling scattered can become a way of life. Such mechanical behavior may not be easy to change.

ADRENALIN ADDICTION—
AN UNHEALTHY WORK HABIT

Adrenalin, the "flight or fight" hormone, is produced by the body during emergencies. It's a wonderful hormone to have coursing through your body if you are being chased by a bear. Your heart pounds furiously, breathing becomes more rapid, and your blood pressure rises. You can experience the same physiological changes during a crisis at work.

Many people create pressure for themselves because it makes them feel important and gives them excitement and challenge. In fact, they often set the fires they later have to extinguish. The problem is that sitting behind a desk allows you no opportunity to burn off excess adrenalin. An accumulation can lead to high blood pressure, ulcers, and other ailments—making adrenalin addiction one of the most unhealthy work habits and one of the best reasons for wise time management.

YOUR COMFORT ZONE—
AN OLD SHOE?

A comfort zone is a psychological zone above and below which we feel anxious. One of the major barriers to good time management is a desire to stay within our comfort zones.

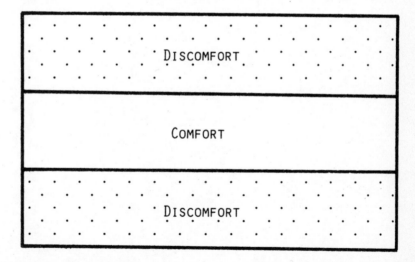

We have comfort zones for many behaviors, such as how much authority we feel comfortable having, how much responsibility we are willing to delegate, how long we procrastinate on projects before beginning, how much responsibility we are willing to assume, and how cluttered we allow our desks to become before cleaning them off. These comfort zones are comprised of habits that are as comfortable as old shoes. We hate to give them up even though they are worn out. Getting used to newer, more productive ways of doing things will require some initial discomfort and change in routine—a bit like breaking in a pair of new shoes.

HOW TO EXPAND YOUR COMFORT ZONE

To expand your comfort zone means to grow as a person, to reach even greater potential, to avoid stagnating in self-made ruts, and to have a more exciting, satisfying life.

In order to break out of your traditional ways of doing things, which might not be time-effective, first be aware of your habits. In the first chapter, you began to examine your attitudes toward time. Continue that self-examination. Keeping a *time log,* as suggested in Chapter 4, enables you to better understand how you manage time and to identify your patterns of wasting it. A shortcut to gaining awareness of your problem areas is to ask your co-workers what they've observed about the way you handle your time.

Next, challenge yourself to change. Emerson wisely instructs us to, "Do the thing you fear and the death of fear is certain." For example, it may be comfortable for you to sit quietly in a staff meeting that is dragging on and on because you are fearful of speaking in front of a group or afraid of asserting yourself by asking if the meeting could get on target again. Speak up anyway; the next time will be a little easier, and the more you express yourself with people, the more self-confidence you will enjoy. If you resist delegating, delegate anyway and get used to exercising more authority.

Now that you've identified some of your problem areas and have started to challenge yourself to change, be consistent with your follow-through by applying the following *habit-control action plan.*

YOUR HABIT-CONTROL ACTION PLAN

It often takes about three weeks to break a habit. Allow yourself at least that long to uproot your old behavior and replace it with a more effective pattern. Choose one bad time-management habit you have, such as procrastinating on projects or cluttering up your desk. Decide *now* to change that habit. The longer you postpone changing, the more likely you are to forget about it. You may have learned to be comfortable with your discomfort; but remember, even a carpeted rut is still a rut.

1. *Write down the habit you want to change.*

EXAMPLE: Working at a disorganized desk.

HABIT: _____

_____

2. *Write your goal in finished form.* Focus on the results, not on the process. For example, rather than having as a goal, "Cleaning my desk," have as a goal, "Desk clean and organized." Visualizing the end results will keep you motivated. Many times the process you must undergo is not that pleasant. Doesn't it feel better to picture yourself sitting at a well-organized desk rather than to picture yourself cleaning it? Take a few moments now and write your goal in terms of your overall objective.

EXAMPLE: I have my desk clean and organized.

GOAL:_____

_____

3. *Make your results measurable.* How will you know when your desk is cleaned and organized exactly the way you want it? Write down how you will measure your results.

EXAMPLE: I have only one thing on my desk at a time, and a place for everything.

I WILL HAVE ACHIEVED MY GOAL WHEN:_____

_____

4. *List all the problems you create with your habit.*

EXAMPLE: When my desk is cluttered, my attention is scattered and I don't think as clearly.

PROBLEM:_____

_____

PROBLEM:_____

_____

PROBLEM:_____

_____

5. *List all the benefits of changing your habit.*

EXAMPLE: With a clean desk, it's easier for me to concentrate for extended periods of time.

BENEFIT:_____

_____

BENEFIT:_____

_____

BENEFIT:_____

_____

6. *Exaggerate the results.* If you previously have been messy, become *super*-organized. If you used to be late to meetings, for three weeks be *super*-early. If you used to procrastinate, finish *well before* deadlines. If nonassertion has been your style, become *super*-assertive. Since there is a tendency for many people to backslide, if you become a *super* time manager, you should come out just about right.

7. *Allow no slippage.* The second you catch yourself granting a stay of execution to your old habit, stop what you are doing, take a deep breath, and begin

with your new pattern. For example, if your goal is "Clean desk," and you realize that you are accumulating clutter, *stop*. Clean your work area immediately and begin anew. It may take a few minutes, but you will save time in the long run by training yourself to keep your desk organized in the first place.

8. *Enlist the support of others*. People probably will notice right away that you are doing things differently. Their reactions may surprise you. You might be a threat to them at first because you are demonstrating that it *is* possible to be more organized. This may make them question their own methods; they could try to sabotage your efforts by interrupting you or trying to entice you away from your objectives. Be firm and consistent. Explain what you are doing and ask for their support. Show them that you value your time and they'll respect it as well.

9. *Use affirmations*. Write a positive statement of your goal on a 3x5 card and put it on your desk. For example, "I have a clean, well-organized desk," or, "I finish things fully," or, "I am a decisive, assertive person." Stop now and write down an affirmation or two that you can use today.

AFFIRMATION:_____

_____

AFFIRMATION:_____

_____

10. *Reward yourself*. Rewards are far more effective than criticism. Focus on what you have accomplished toward your goal, not on where you've slipped. If you have a speech to write, reward yourself for having started writing it and celebrate having finished each section. Treat yourself to a meal out or heap lavish praise on yourself. After you've given the speech, allow yourself an even bigger reward for a job well done.

11. *Visually rehearse your new behavior*. See yourself beginning new projects on time, finishing paperwork by the end of the day, dealing competently with problems as they arise, being on time, working on a clean desk, and enjoying more free time than ever before. Stop now, sit back, and take a minute or two to visualize your results.

12. *Be positive*. Don't let memories of past failures interfere with your progress today. Avoid using words such as *try, wish,* and *hope*; they imply a willingness to compromise. Instead of saying that you are trying to start new projects on time, state, "I start new projects on time." Avoid using absolutes such as *always* and *never*. Promising yourself that you *never again* will let your desk get cluttered doesn't allow for unseen circumstances. Be firm with yourself, but be reasonable as well.

1. Write down the habit you want to change.
2. Write your goal in finished form.
3. Make your results measurable.
4. List all the problems you create with your habit.
5. To build motivation for changing, list all the benefits of breaking the habit.
6. Exaggerate the results; for example, if you have previously been disorganized, become *super*-organized for three weeks until you have established the new pattern.
7. Allow no slippage.
8. Enlist the support of others.
9. Use positive affirmations.
10. Reward yourself.
11. Visually rehearse your new behavior; see yourself the way you want to be.
12. Be positive; don't let past failures interfere with your progress today.

Your Action Plan

A. Pick a troublesome time-management habit that you have and follow the twelve steps for breaking a bad habit.
B. Scan the contents in this book; identify the area of time management in which you need the most help. Turn directly to that chapter and read it.

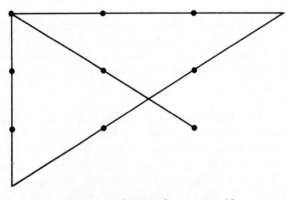

Answer to the puzzle on page 10.

"You cannot run away from a weakness; you must some time fight it out or perish; and if that be so, why not now, and where you stand?"
—Robert Louis Stevenson

"There's only one corner of the universe you can be certain of improving, and that's your own self."
—Aldous Huxley

3

ELEPHANT HUNTING—SET GOALS AND BAG THE BIG GAME!

OBJECTIVES

When you finish this chapter, you will be able to:

- Identify your long-term professional and personal goals to obtain a clearer sense of direction
- Target high-payoff activities in your business and private life
- Plot priorities on a payoff/priority grid
- Break your goals into measurable steps
- Apply the 80/20 principle to determine the right thing on which to be focusing
- Write an effective to-do list
- Distinguish between being *efficient* and being *effective*

It's hard to aim the rifle if you can't see the target. Once you know where you're going, you can focus your energy and concentration on your goal and get there faster and easier.

ELEPHANT HUNTING

An important key to being successful with time management is to make elephant hunting your highest priority. This means to go after your big, high-payoff goals every day and to minimize the time you spend stomping on ants, those trivial details that take up so much time.

There will always be ants and elephants in our lives. Unfortunately, many of us who are elephant hunters at heart end up stomping ants. The danger lies in making a career of ant stomping. We tend to go after ants instead of elephants because we get a quicker kill and a higher body count. But remember, killing ants doesn't put much meat on the table. Hunting elephants will.

DON'T STOMP ANTS
WHEN ELEPHANTS ARE COMING OVER THE WALLS!!

IDENTIFY YOUR ELEPHANTS

The way to determine the right elephants for you to be hunting is to apply the *80/20 principle*, which states that approximately 20 percent of what you do yields 80 percent of the results and, conversely, 80 percent of what you do yields 20 percent of the results. The 80/20 principle was first described by Vilfredo Pareto, an Italian economist, who observed that 20 percent of the people in Italy owned 80 percent of the wealth. Examples of the 80/20 principle can be seen in most areas of our professional and private lives.

- If you are in sales, 20 percent of your customers often yield about 80 percent of the dollar value of your sales. Looking for trends in sales, identifying that lucrative 20 percent, and allocating your time accordingly would be hunting elephants.
- In administration and supervision, 20 percent of your employees often do 80 percent of the work. Giving recognition and motivating the appropriate employees will give you a very high return on your invested time.
- In customer relations, about 20 percent of the customers make 80 percent of the complaints. Keep your perspective and don't let the significant few influence the service you give your other customers.

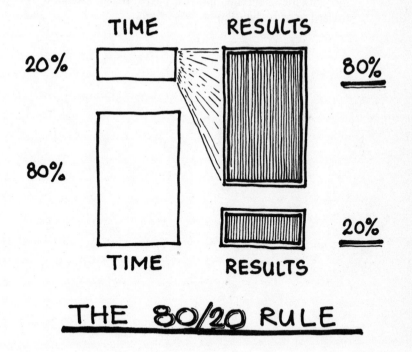

THE 80/20 RULE

- Twenty percent of the newspaper has 80 percent of the news. Skim the rest.
- Twenty percent of your to-do list and your paperwork yields 80 percent of the value. Learn to recognize and concentrate on those items and finish the others as quickly as possible with the minimum standards required.

- In meetings and during telephone calls, 20 percent of the time you spend nets 80 percent of the results. Have you ever noticed that when meetings and phone calls are almost over and you still have several important points to cover how you can wrap it all up very quickly?
- Housework, the bane of many of us, surrenders nicely to the 80/20 principle. Twenty percent of the places in the house, such as hallways and entranceways, get 80 percent of the dirt. Identify where most of the dirt collects and clean there. Have you ever noticed how much cleaning you can do in the hour before company comes? Save time and concentrate on the high-payoff cleaning. Once in a while, you might want to clean the entire house, but most of the time it's not necessary.

What are *your* elephants at work? Which activities give you the highest payoff? What gives you the most personal fulfillment? What can you do to serve your organization more? By making the company more effective, you enhance your career as well, because you and the organization have a partnership.

What are your elephants in your private life? Do you want to become independently wealthy? Improve your health? Become a more positive person? Learn new skills? Spend more time with loved ones? Communicate more clearly? In order to hunt elephants, you first have to identify them.

Take a few moments now and identify the high-payoff targets in your life. Use the worksheets on the following pages. Be sure to list the action steps that contribute toward your realization of those goals.

IDENTIFY THE HIGH-PAYOFF TARGETS
IN YOUR PROFESSIONAL LIFE

HIGH-PAYOFF TARGETS

ACTION STEPS

Example:

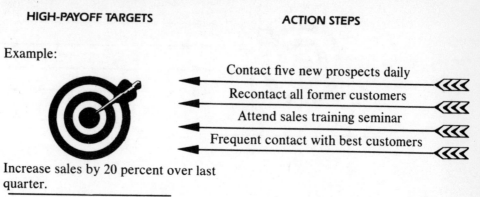

Contact five new prospects daily

Recontact all former customers

Attend sales training seminar

Frequent contact with best customers

Increase sales by 20 percent over last quarter.

TARGET

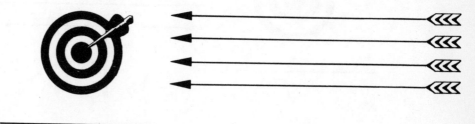

TARGET

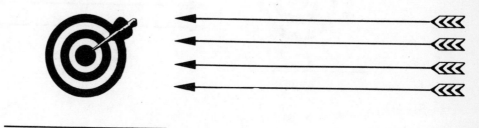

TARGET

HIGH-PAYOFF TARGETS   **ACTION STEPS**

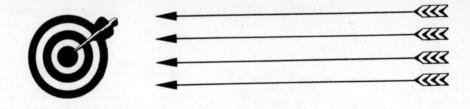

_____
TARGET

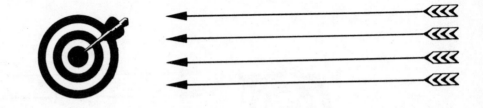

_____
TARGET

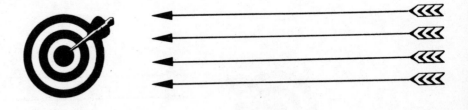

_____
TARGET

IDENTIFY THE HIGH-PAYOFF TARGETS
IN YOUR PERSONAL LIFE

HIGH-PAYOFF TARGETS   **ACTION STEPS**

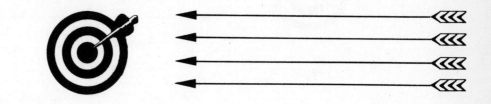

TARGET

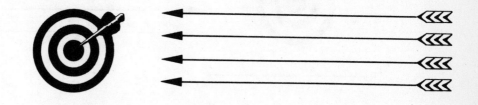

TARGET

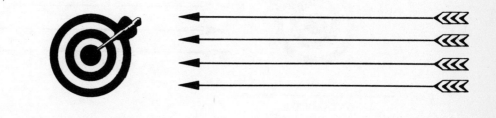

TARGET

HIGH-PAYOFF TARGETS   **ACTION STEPS**

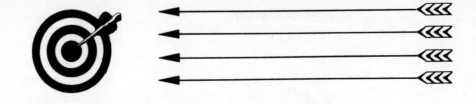

TARGET

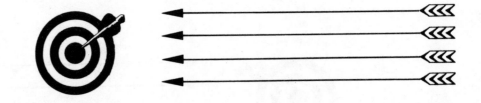

TARGET

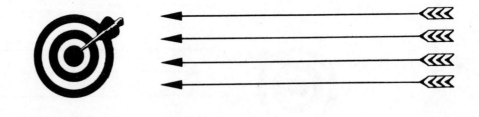

TARGET

REDUCING TIME SPENT ON
LOW-PAYOFF ITEMS AT WORK

As you complete the following exercise, imagine that you can spend only half the usual time on your job, but are required to accomplish as much as when you were a full-time employee. This is a good way to be objective about your job. It may be that many of the activities you do are not that significant in terms of getting your job done.

**List low-payoff items
that you do at work.**

**What can you do to spend
less time on these items?**

ITEM:_____

_____

ITEM:_____

_____

ITEM:_____

_____

**List low-payoff items
that you do at work.**

**What can you do to spend
less time on these items?**

ITEM:_____   _____

_____   _____

_____

_____

_____

ITEM:_____   _____

_____   _____

_____

_____

_____

REDUCING TIME SPENT ON
LOW-PAYOFF ITEMS IN
YOUR PERSONAL LIFE

Ask yourself, "If I only had three months to live, how would I spend my personal time?" Asking this question gives you the jolt you need to help you focus your energy and gain better control of your life. For example, low-payoff personal time might be watching too much television. To spend less time watching television, you might want to target your TV time by deciding exactly what you are going to watch; don't sit passively and take whatever program comes next.

List low-payoff items that you do in your personal life.	What can you do to spend less time on these items?
ITEM:_____	_____
_____	_____
	_____
	_____
	_____
ITEM:_____	_____
_____	_____
	_____
	_____
	_____
ITEM:_____	_____
_____	_____
	_____
	_____
	_____

**List low-payoff items that
you do in your personal life.**

**What can you do to spend
less time on these items?**

ITEM:_____   _____

_____   _____

        _____

        _____

        _____

ITEM:_____   _____

_____   _____

        _____

        _____

        _____

GOING ON AN ELEPHANT-HUNTING SAFARI

Chances are that you routinely set priorities, but do you set the *right* priorities on the right activities by keeping your long-term objectives clearly in mind? Do you spend some time every day working toward achieving your important life goals or do you simply give high priority to items that demand the most attention? The key to setting priorities, the order in which you must accomplish things, is to ask yourself, "What is my payoff for doing this activity? How does it fit in with my long-term objectives, with the overall direction of a particular project or with my career?"

Often when we think about setting priorities, we lose track of the true direction we should be taking. We ask ourselves, "What is the most *urgent* thing for me to be doing? What is the next most urgent thing?" The items we think can wait often have the most significant payoff for us, perhaps not immediately, but in the future. For example, everyone in my seminars agrees that brushing our teeth daily is top priority, but they are not sure if exercising should have top priority. Most people are more concerned about halitosis than heart attacks! Often we declare that we value certain things, but live our lives differently. Most people would agree that goal-setting is very important, but do you allocate time to spend on setting goals?

On the following grid, *payoff* refers to value; *priority* refers to urgency. The uppermost left square is 1A; the lowermost right square is 3C, and so on. Low-payoff, low-priority items, those on which you should never work as long as you have something else to do, go in square 3C. Activities on which you should always work, no matter what, go in square 1A. Not only are they important, but they are urgent as well. With this in mind, where would you plot the following activities?

- Washing your car when it looks like rain
- Changing the oil in your car when the red light is on
- Brushing your teeth when you haven't brushed them in three days
- Organizing the files in your office
- Cleaning your desk
- Exercising
- Buying a birthday card for your best friend
- Having business cards printed

Think of examples of high-payoff and low-payoff activities from your own life and assign each item a coordinate on the grid.

PRIORITY

	A (DO NOW)	B (DO SOON)	C (CAN WAIT)
1 **High**			
P A Y O F F **2** **Medium** **Value**			
3 **Low** **Value**			

Many people have trouble working on their 1C entries, which are valuable for them but have no urgency. These elephants get neglected because people often prioritize by urgency, regardless of payoff. Examples of important but not urgent 1C elephants are long-range planning, self-improvement, personal organization, communicating on a deeper level with people, and spending more quality time with family and friends.

Focus on doing your 1As, 1Bs, and 1Cs. If you must handle trivia, do the low-payoff items as quickly as possible with the minimum quality required. For example, jot down the answers to memos in the margins of the memos and send them back.

Start every day by deciding which elephant you will hunt that day and block out sufficient time to work on it. If the project is large, break it down into smaller units. Work on important things early in the day. If something unexpected comes up later, you will already have finished your high-payoff items.

HOW TO DEAL WITH HIGH-PAYOFF ACTIVITIES

1. Build your day around high-payoff activities; schedule less important items for the time left over.
2. Stay focused. Put distractions aside and keep the end results in mind.
3. Set deadlines. Make them specific.
4. Divide projects into smaller units. "By the inch, it's a cinch."
5. Get help. Sometimes you can't do it alone.
6. Use your peak times. Attack difficult things when you are mentally sharpest.
7. Reward yourself. Keep yourself motivated.
8. Make a commitment. Full speed ahead!

1. Delegate them. Let someone else help you to free up your time.
2. Trade them with someone else. Swap chores such as answering the phone and doing errands.
3. Systematize them. Use check lists and get a good filing system.
4. Lower your standards. What is the minimum acceptable level of quality with which you can get by?
5. Ignore them. Some things are better left undone (reading junk mail, attending certain luncheon meetings, etc.).
6. Pay someone else to do them. Eat in a restaurant or hire a housekeeper.
7. Group them together. Return calls or do all paperwork at a set time.

EXTINGUISH THE ANTS

Sometimes ants are not merely annoying little creatures, but destructive, poisonous fire ants that deliver a powerful sting. Or they may be army ants that storm the countryside devouring everything in sight and building bridges made from the bodies of their fellow ants. How can you focus on your elephants when trivia is about to consume you?

Delay the ants. When a long column of real ants is winding its way toward you, there are things you can do to remove the urgency of the problem. You can kill the scouts or draw a line across the trails to disrupt the scent the leaders have left for the others.

Similar strategies can be applied to projects. You may not have to deal with everything at once. Break your projects into parts and work on each part just enough to remove it from a *do now* status to a *do later* status. Delegate whenever possible.

Group your ants. Herd your ants together and deal with them one after another during a special time you have set aside each day. This way, they aren't trailing in one by one to disrupt you.

Stop doing the ants. Some people like to stomp ants because it makes them look busy and feel important. They mistake activity for accomplishment. It is better to work on the right thing slowly than on the wrong thing quickly.

One man I know gave up doing *all* of his paperwork. He discovered that he didn't need to do most of it. When the items were really important, people would follow up on them and ask him again for his attention; in these cases, he would comply. You might not want to pursue such a radical approach to your trivia, especially if you're not the boss, but surely there are areas in your job that you can eliminate. For example, perhaps you photocopy papers that someone else already has copies of.

Which low-payoff activities (ants) can you delay, group, or stop doing? Make a list below.

EXAMPLE: Running unnecessary errands, excessive time on junk mail, excessive socializing, procrastinating, shuffling papers.

ANT:_____

_____

ANT:_____

_____

ANT:_____

_____

ANT:_____

_____

ANT:_____

_____

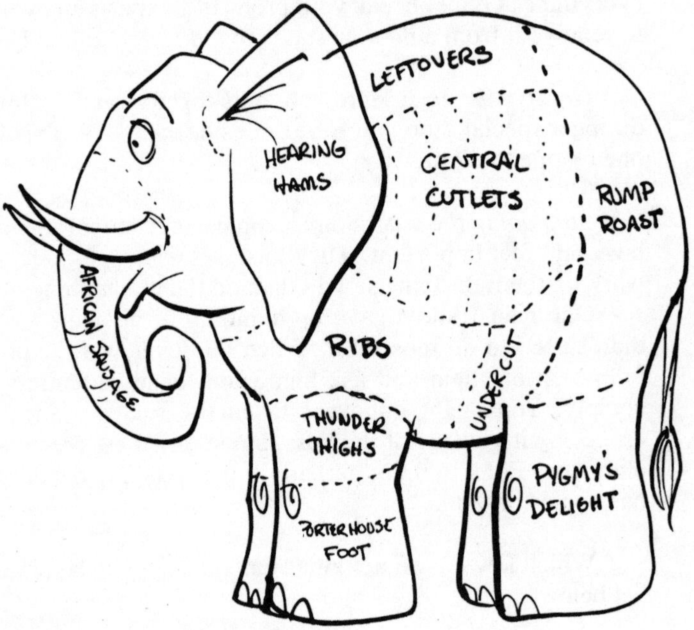

SELECT THE PART OF THE ELEPHANT
THAT YOU WANT TO HUNT EACH DAY

You might not capture the entire elephant on one trip, so go for parts of it by breaking your goal into smaller, do-able steps with measurable outcomes.

YOUR GOAL

_____

_____

Do you really want this goal? ____YES ____NO

How much time are you willing to devote each day toward realizing this goal? TIME:_____

If you aren't willing to put in even a minimal amount of time every day until you attain your goal, move on to another goal.

Do you deserve this goal? ____YES ____NO

Do you have any anxiety, nervousness, or hesitancy about being successful? ____YES ____NO

If yes, take a few minutes now and explore those feelings.

_____

_____

_____

Now that you have examined your feelings, are you sincerely willing to make a commitment to achieving the goal? ____YES ____NO

If Yes, let's go on. If No, choose another goal with which you are willing to work.

You are now ready to plot the steps to follow in order to achieve your goal. For example, if your goal is to have one hour of quiet time each day, your challenge is to eliminate unnecessary interruptions. A barrier might be lack of assertiveness on your part. Possible action steps would be: Explain to people that you must have quiet time every day; inform people as to the best time to speak with you; be willing to say "No" more frequently; read a book on assertion; take an assertiveness training course.

PLAN TO SUCCEED

In the consulting I've done with thousands of people, they've all declared that they are planning to succeed in their lives. No one admits to consciously planning to fail and yet many people go through life without a plan. If you are one of these people who fail to plan, who do not set goals for yourself or write daily to-do lists, you may be planning to fail.

Get in the habit of writing a *to-do list* every day. Use the following guidelines.

1. Be realistic and aware of the limitations of your time frame. Just as you can fit only so many marbles in a jar, you can fit only so many activities in your day. Don't overschedule. You'll feel much better when you finish 10 out of 10 items instead of 10 out of 20. What you leave undone can tire you; what you accomplish energizes you.
2. Allow a time cushion. Don't cram every minute with activities. Provide for the unexpected such as clients being late to appointments or projects taking longer than you estimated.
3. Review your list every morning before beginning work. Keep it in sight. Refer to it periodically throughout the day to keep your objectives in mind.
4. If you do something during the day that is not on your list, add it. At the end of the day, you can look back over your list and realize that you accomplished more than you had originally intended.
5. Before doing each item on your list, ask, "Why me?" If someone else can or should be doing that item, turn it over to her or him.
6. Group related activities. For example, if you have an important call to make, make your other calls while you are still at the phone.
7. Hunt an elephant, or part of an elephant, each day. Focus on payoff instead of urgency. Do something every day to move you closer to your goals. Just dreaming is not enough!

The following forms, A through D, outline a successful action plan for you. The forms for your use are in the appendix of this book. Use them faithfully and succeed!

HOW TO PLAN A SUCCESSFUL TO-DO LIST

1. Get in the habit of writing a to-do list every day.
2. Be realistic and aware of the limitations of your time frame.
3. Don't overschedule.
4. Allow a time cushion.
5. Review your list every morning.
6. Add more items as you do them.
7. Before doing each item, ask, "Why me?" Delegate when possible.
8. Group related activities.
9. Hunt an elephant, or part of an elephant, each day.

FORM A—ACTION ITEMS

1. As things come up that need to be done during the week, list them on this form.
2. Determine the payoff (importance) and priority (urgency) of each item.
3. Refer to this list when you are planning your daily to-do list, Form C.

week of: _____		**a**
goals: (a) _____		
(b) _____		
(c) _____		

action items:

payoff · hi p.o. = 1; med p.o. = 2; lo p.o. = 3
priority · hi pri = A; med pri = B; lo pri = C

	p.o.	pri	
1			
2			
3			
4			
5			
6			
7			
8			
9			
10			
11			
12			
13			
14			
15			
16			
17			
18			
19			
20			
21			
22			
23			
24			
25			

1. Fill in your committed time first, such as appointments and meetings.
2. Note previously established deadlines.
3. Allocate time to work on upcoming deadlines.
4. Note other major items to which you want to devote time.

successful week of:

b

	monday	tuesday	wednesday	thursday
7				
9				
11				
noon				
1				
3				
5				
7				

	friday	saturday	sunday	activities to be scheduled:
7				
9				
11				
noon				
1				
3				
5				
7				

FORM C—DAILY SCHEDULE

1. Each day, refer to Form A, the master list of action items that need doing. Choose the items on the list that are most appropriate on which to work for that day.
2. List them in the "action flow" section and note their payoffs and priorities.
3. Schedule these items into their appropriate time slots:
   a. Be sure that you have planned to work on at least one major high-payoff item every day.
   b. Schedule your most difficult work during your periods of peak mental effectiveness.
   c. Allow time cushions throughout your day so that you are not overly pressured.

c

day: _____

goals: (a) _____
 (b) _____
 (c) _____

action items:

payoff - hi p.o. = 1; med p.o. = 2; lo p.o. = 3
priority - hi pri = A; med pri = B; lo pri = C

p.o.	pri	

phone calls:

action flow

7:30	
8:00	
8:30	
9:00	
9:30	
10:00	
10:30	
11:00	
11:30	
noon	
12:30	
1:00	
1:30	
2:00	
2:30	
3:00	
3:30	
4:00	
4:30	
5:00	
5:30	
6:00	
6:30	
7:00	

1. Write down on the slanted line the activity or project for which you want to develop an action flow. It might be a large project or a major activity on which you have been procrastinating.
2. Record on the horizontal lines running from the slanted lines the details that must be done regarding that activity or project.
3. In the small square on each horizontal line, write the priority of doing that detail.
4. Use the detail list column to relist the details in the order in which they should be done.
5. Use the additional slanted lines if required for a more thorough analysis of the project.

priority -
hi pri = A
med pri = B
lo pri = C

activity   activity   activity

action flow   date _____   d

activity	activity	activity
detail list	detail list	detail list
1.	1.	1.
2.	2.	2.
3.	3.	3.
4.	4.	4.
5.	5.	5.
6.	6.	6.
7.	7.	7.
8.	8.	8.

Let's get rich. If I had a hundred bills in my hand, ninety-eight of them $1 bills and two of them $100 bills, and a whirlwind blew them all through the room, what would be your strategy for picking them up?

If you are thinking in terms of being *efficient,* you would think, I'll pick up the money closest to me and work my way toward the two $100 dollar bills.

If you are thinking in terms of being *effective,* you would ask, Where did the hundreds go? You would head for those even if they had blown across the room. Maybe you'd only get the $100 bills and someone else would get all the rest. However, at best, the other person would have $98, while you'd have $200, plus whatever else you picked up afterward.

Know your objective and go for that! If your goal is making money and maximizing your return, go for the hundreds. If you are unfortunately caught up in the *busyness* of being efficient, go for the dollar bills. Being efficient is doing the right thing within a given time frame. Being effective is doing the *right* thing right. Being effective as opposed to being efficient means the difference between hunting elephants and stomping ants.

Your Action Plan

A. Identify the high-payoff elephants in your professional life. List the activities to achieve these goals. Use the worksheets in this chapter.
B. Identify the high-payoff elephants in your personal life. List the action steps to accomplish these goals.
C. List the low-payoff items you do at work and at home. Write down ways you can spend less time on these items.
D. Fill in high-payoff/low-payoff activities on your priority/payoff grid.
E. Write to-do lists for the upcoming week. Use the forms provided.

QUOTES TO CONSIDER

"First say to yourself what you would be; and then what you have to do."

—Epictetus

"Man is not the creature of circumstances. Circumstances are the creatures of men."

—Benjamin Disraeli

"Plan for the future because that's where you are going to spend the rest of your life."

—Mark Twain

4

KEEPING A
TIME LOG

OBJECTIVES

When you finish this chapter, you will be able to:

- Begin to recognize your specific patterns of wasting time
- Estimate how long it will take you to accomplish certain tasks
- Compute your percentage of time effectiveness on any activity
- Schedule more realistically
- Avoid time crunches

"Where did my time go?" "Oh, no! I'm late again!" "I worked so hard all day and yet, I feel like I haven't done anything!"

You're already aware of the *obvious* time wasters which plague you, but do you realize all the little ways that time can drain away? Keeping a time log provides evidence of exactly where your time is going and why.

It would be an excellent thing to log your time every day for three weeks, but in my experience, most people don't keep up with it for that long. I'm not going to ask you to keep a log for three weeks straight, but I am going to insist that you keep a log for *one* day a week for three weeks. This is the minimum dosage with which you can get by and still gain insights into your time slippage.

WHEN TO BE PESSIMISTIC

I'm a great believer in being positive, but when it comes to estimating how long it will take you to do something, I encourage you to be more pessimistic. Almost all my clients underestimate how long it will take them to do their work. This explains who so many of them feel pressured and face so much crisis management.

Have you ever noticed how a half-hour project often takes twice as long as you imagined it would? This is probably because you estimated only the *actual working time,* and did not take into account your preparation and think time, or your need to reflect, recheck, and revise. Your time log will force you to confront the difference between what you *think* is going on, and what is actually happening regarding how you spend your time.

A SAMPLE TIME LOG

Although the sample *time log* (opposite) covers only one day, we can already see patterns emerging. Six of the nine activities in the log were caused directly by the person keeping the log, *not* by outside influences. This person can become much more effective time-wise by working on *inner* causes of wasted time!

time log

time	time invested		activity	% effectiveness · how can I handle it more effectively next time?
	est.	act.		
9 AM	10 M.	15 M.	Reviewing Day's Plan	67%: Distracted by papers on desk. Solution: Clear desk before I start.
9:15 AM	20 M.	50 M.	Writing Letter	40%: Bogged down in perfectionism on how to word it. Next time force myself to go on and write whole 1st draft at rapid pace and see if it is good enough.
10:05 AM	5 M.	12 M.	Call Jones Account	42%: Got off on tangent. Solution: Stick to phone call priority list.
10:17 AM	15 M.	30 M.	Coffee Break	50%: I rationalized that since I started my break at 10:17 instead of the official 10:15 I deserved a few extra minutes that stretched with socializing. Solution: Use more discipline.
10:47 AM	5 M.	13 M.	Call Wilson	39%: Same phone troubles as above. Solution: Stick to phone call priority list.
11 AM	30 M.	45 M.	Sales Meeting	67%: Delay in starting meeting by 5 min. Many of us were too wordy. Solution: Clarify starting time and how much time we each have to speak.
11:45 AM	5 M.	15 M.	Call Thompson Co.	33%: Thompson's rep. not in—Called friend Jerry to see about tickets to concert. Talked about everything. Solution: Stick to priorities.
12:00	60 M.	90 M.	Lunch	67%: Slow service—missed 1 PM appointment. Solution: Change restaurants or allow more time.
4:45 PM	15 M.	25 M.	Planning for tomorrow	60%: Morgan dropped by to set golf plans—too many phone interruptions. Solution: Block interruptions.

HOW TO LOG YOUR TIME

Personally, I don't enjoy keeping time logs, but I do them anyway because I gain enormous insights from them. Initially, keeping a time log will slow you down because you have to stop and record every activity before you do it, including how long you think it will take you to finish it, how long it actually took, and your recommendations to yourself for being more time-effective the next time. In keeping a time log, you pay the price of short-term discomfort for long-term reward.

Decide now which days in the following three weeks you will keep your log.

DATE, WEEK 1:_____

DATE, WEEK 2:_____

DATE, WEEK 3:_____

Using the time log in Appendix II of this book, do the following:

1. Keep your time log with you throughout the day so you can be as accurate as possible.
2. Record each activity that you are about to begin. Then record your estimate of how long it will take you to finish.
3. When you have completed the activity, record the actual time it took you.
4. In the far right column, compute the percentage of your effectiveness. To obtain this percentage, divide your estimated time by the actual time it took you to finish the item. Then multiply this number by 100.
5. In the percentage column, evaluate what went wrong and how you can handle that task and similar tasks more effectively the next time.

time log

time	time invested est.	act.	activity	% effectiveness • how can I handle it more effectively next time?

HOW TO EVALUATE YOUR TIME LOG

Look for patterns of good time usage and time *wastage*. Answer the following:

How much of your day was spent:

Handling interruptions   DAY 1: _____ DAY 2: _____ DAY 3: _____

Procrastinating   DAY 1: _____ DAY 2: _____ DAY 3: _____

On the telephone   DAY 1: _____ DAY 2: _____ DAY 3: _____

Handling crises   DAY 1: _____ DAY 2: _____ DAY 3: _____

Planning   DAY 1: _____ DAY 2: _____ DAY 3: _____

In meetings   DAY 1: _____ DAY 2: _____ DAY 3: _____

Other: _____   DAY 1: _____ DAY 2: _____ DAY 3: _____

Other: _____   DAY 1: _____ DAY 2: _____ DAY 3: _____

Other: _____   DAY 1: _____ DAY 2: _____ DAY 3: _____

Time spent on high-payoff items vs. low-payoff items:

High-payoff items   DAY 1: _____ DAY 2: _____ DAY 3: _____

Low-payoff items   DAY 1: _____ DAY 2: _____ DAY 3: _____

Are you satisfied with how your time was spent? If not, turn to the chapter in this book which addresses your problem.

YOUR ACTION PLAN

Begin your time log first thing tomorrow morning.

5

MASTER YOUR WORKING ENVIRONMENT

OBJECTIVES

When you finish this chapter, you will be able to:

- Use your workspace as your closest ally in your war against wasting time
- Maintain a desk that is clean and organized
- Designate parking places for all office and personal items so you can locate them at a moment's notice
- Handle paperwork quickly and effectively
- Streamline your files

Raise your IQ—organize your workspace! Because you spend so many hours of your career in your work environment, it pays you highly to keep it clear of clutter and distractions. When your work area is clean and organized, you concentrate better, work faster, and remember longer. When you are under less pressure, you are more creative and you increase your problem-solving abilities.

TAKE AN OBJECTIVE LOOK AT YOUR WORKSPACE

	YES	NO
1. Does your desk grow paper?	——	——
2. Is your desk a clean working surface that helps you focus your energy on the task at hand?	——	——
3. Do you get a positive feeling when you approach your desk?	——	——
4. Is your desk such a mess that you invent ways to avoid it all together?	——	——
5. Is your file cabinet a black hole that sucks in paper, notes, articles, documents, and endless items you have duplicated?	——	——
6. Is your filing system a streamlined, orderly one that supports you in getting your job done?	——	——
7. Is the physical appearance of your work space uncluttered, cheerful, and light?	——	——
8. Is your work space conducive to clear, creative thinking?	——	——
9. Is your office a pit that would give a Spanish inquisitor ideas?	——	——

YOUR DESK—THE NUCLEUS OF YOUR WORK AREA

Since most of your business activity emanates from your desk, it is the perfect place to start organizing.

Why do desks get so disorganized in the first place? It might be because you have so many important things to do that you are afraid that if you put them out of sight, you might forget or misplace them. Meanwhile, more important items come to your attention, as well as assorted notes, and they get piled on top of all the others.

All of those little pieces of paper cry out to you, nagging, "Do me first!" "No, no, do *me* first! I'm an emergency!" "But I'm an emergency, too. I was due yesterday!" "You promised your boss that you'd do me first and if you don't, you'll be sorry!"

Trying to work under these conditions can be exhausting. It takes valuable energy to ignore all that paper while you are attempting to give your full attention to what you are doing at the moment.

BEFORE

SCOOP EVERYTHING OFF YOUR DESK

Just look at it, devoid of clutter. Does it feel good? Is it refreshing to see it this way? Or does it make you feel nervous? If it makes you uncomfortable, you may be one of those people who equates messiness with productivity. The two are not the same. If you work at a cluttered desk, you will tend to have a cluttered mind.

Now return your most recent project to the top of your desk. The project might include several file folders, a book or two, and some forms. Don't confuse all these items with a messy desk, provided that they are related to your project. The point is to be working on one thing at a time, and as much as possible to have just one thing at a time upon which to focus. This helps you concentrate better and think more clearly.

THE TASK
AT HAND

AFTER

Now what will you do with all the other papers you just scooped off your desk? And what do you do when the incoming paperwork is greater than your ability to process it?

HARVEST TIME ON THE PAPER FARM

Get rid of that unwieldy crop of paper by making a list on one piece of paper that indicates where you put each item. Put this map in a top desk drawer.

Begin a *dump drawer*. Designate one of the lower drawers of your desk to be a dump drawer. Into this drawer put all low-payoff, low-priority items such as flyers, brochures, newspapers, and other mail that isn't time-critical. Let these items ripen in your dump drawer for a month or so, then dump them.

One afternoon a month, or the last hour on Fridays when you don't feel like beginning any major projects, plan a *trivia session*. Go through your dump drawer and handle whatever has accumulated. Scan the items quickly and decide whether to toss them out, let them ripen further, delegate them, or do them. You will discover that about 90 percent of what goes into your dump drawer can be thrown out.

Create a *message center*. I'm a sucker for messages. Whenever someone puts a note on my desk, my curiosity gets the best of me. I have to stop what I'm doing and read it. Knowing this tendency of mine, I've developed a message center, a special place in the other room where I've asked people to put my non-urgent messages. This way, I'm not interrupted by all those little odds and ends. I check the message center later when I have a few minutes.

Develop a *parking system* for everything that comes into your office, including personal items. Immediately put things in their respective places; you'll find them much easier when you need them again. Decide now where you will park the assorted papers and items that find their way into your office.

Files: Which will you keep near your desk?

_____

Which files will you store in the archives?

_____

_____

Desk: What items will you keep on top?

_____

_____

What types of material will you file in your dump drawer?

_____

_____

Messages: Where will you tell others to park low-priority, non-urgent messages that come in for you?

_____

_____

Notices of Important Events and Meetings: Do you have a *month-at-a-glance* calendar for fast, easy reference? YES____ NO____
Do you have a weekly planning guide? YES____ NO____
Do you maintain a daily to-do list? YES____ NO____
Do you maintain a tickler file? (See page 62 for directions on how to start one) YES____ NO____

FILE IT IN THE WASTEBASKET

As much as 80 percent of all paper in most files is never needed. In fact, if you were to throw out most of your files, no one would ever know or care. Naturally, you will want to keep legal documents and resource materials to which you frequently refer, but for everything else, the motto is:

WHEN IN DOUBT... **THROW IT OUT!**

Ask yourself, "If I should need that information again, is there somewhere I can get it with a reasonable amount of effort?" There are enough pack rats in the world; someone is sure to be hanging on to it.

DUMP IT, DELAY IT, DELEGATE IT, DO IT

What you can't dump, *delay*. Often work comes into your office that does not require your immediate attention or a prompt answer. Handle this kind of work when you have a few free minutes. What you can't delay, *delegate*. Break yourself of doing routine things others were hired to do.

What you can't dump or delay or delegate, *do*. By now, you'll see that the amount of work you actually have to do is a small portion of your paperwork.

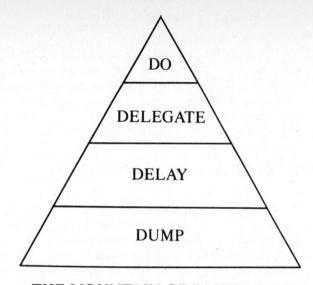

THE MOUNTAIN OF PAPERWORK

SAVE WARM-UP TIME

Often, people open an envelope, glance at the contents, decide that it is worth reading again, then set it aside. The next time they pick it up, they have to refamiliarize themselves with the contents all over again. Save warm-up time! Decide what you want to do with paperwork the first time you look at it. Then do it!

To become aware of how often you handle paper, put a small dot in the upper corner of each piece every time you pick it up to read. Eventually, the paper may look like it has an advanced case of measles! Begin to examine why some of your papers get measles and others remain healthy. Do you avoid processing some paperwork because you don't enjoy working on it? Or because it bores you or is difficult? Or maybe you are just indecisive.

An even more dramatic and permanent cure for the paper shuffle is the *never-fail tear system*. Tear an inch off the top of the paper each time you look at it. This will be powerful incentive to process the work as soon as possible—before it disappears entirely!

DON'T ASK FOR IT

Don't ask for information unless you absolutely need it. Have your staff condense reports when possible. Turn four-page detailed reports into two-page reports that summarize highlights. Or better yet, don't ask for reports if you already know what is going on.

ANSWER CORRESPONDENCE BRIEFLY

If a letter requires a simple answer, jot a reply across it and return it. If it needs a longer reply, dictate only the main points and have your secretary compose the letter. Duplicate correspondence and replies only when absolutely necessary. Chances are the person with whom you are corresponding will keep copies of everything. Don't fall into the habit of C.Y.A. management (cover your—anatomy). This kind of thinking can cover you with an avalanche of paper.

HOW TO SET UP A FILING SYSTEM

Everything you keep costs you time. Storing papers requires filing time, maintenance time, and retrieval time. Important items can get lost in the clutter. You may look at a worthless piece of paper dozens of times while searching for something else. So your goal is to set up your filing system with the emphasis on retrieving information easily, rather than on simply storing paper. That way, you'll increase effectiveness and eliminate stress.

To make sure you have a filing system that suits your needs and is easy to use, follow the simple steps below. Analyze the kinds of information you need to file. Then choose the best method or combination of methods for your filing purposes.

Alphabetical Files. Material is arranged in alphabetical order. File folders have a brief caption designating what kind of material is in each file. A miscellaneous folder is kept in each division from A–Z. Material which has no particular slot is filed alphabetically in the miscellaneous file folder until five or six items have accumulated. Then another file is made. This filing system is good for categorizing a great many pieces of paper.

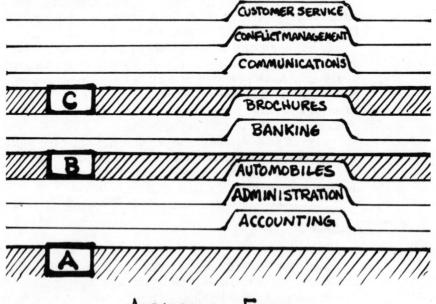

ALPHABETICAL FILES

Topic or subject files. Material is filed alphabetically by topic or subject. One large file is designated for each category rather than several smaller topics. For example, one file is kept on company vehicles rather than three smaller files which deal with licensing, insurance, and repairs. Within the folders, subjects are arranged alphabetically. This type of file might be useful to organize projects where several documents are related to a greater whole.

Geographical files. Material is filed by geographical categories, first by region, then by state and city. Subdivisions are filed alphabetically. Geographical files might be useful for sales managers who need to organize large sales territories.

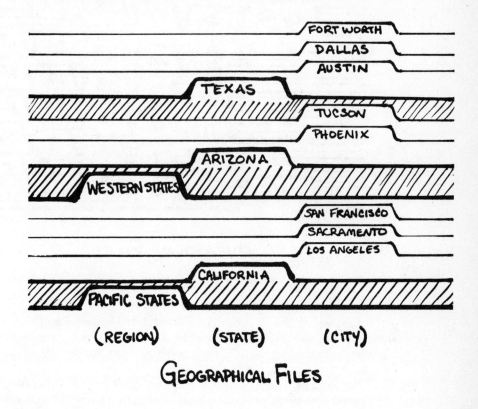

GEOGRAPHICAL FILES

Numerical files. Material is filed according to numbers and then keyed to an alphabetical index. The index shows numerical designations given to each subject or name. Numerical files are used for purchase orders, bank checks, invoices, and company or personal financial records.

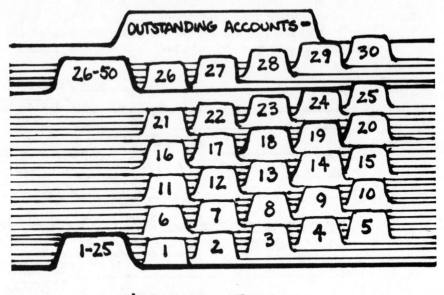

NUMERICAL FILES

Continuous or chronological files. Material is filed chronologically. Everything answered in one day is filed together. This method is usually combined with other methods. It might be useful for people wanting to log important phone calls or expense account records.

Tickler files. These files, used in conjunction with the other filing systems, serve to remind you of upcoming deadlines, things to do, and projects on which to follow through. A tickler file has two major divisions, the first being a set of twelve file folders (one for each month of the year), and the second being *one* set of thirty-one folders for the days of the month. The current month is placed first in the drawer with the days behind it.

At the beginning of each month, transfer items for that month into appropriate daily slots. File work in the tickler file according to when you want to begin it. For example, if you have a report due January 15, file the material under the date you wish to begin. If you have a bill due January 10, file it in the January 7 folder. If the materials are too bulky, slip a note into the slot.

Tickler files can be useful for keeping track of items to which you want to refer later, such as follow-up dates, payments, and birthdays or anniversaries.

Decide *who* will file *what* for *how long.* Once I was consulting in a firm whose employees were complaining about the unwieldy mess of papers in their file cabinets.

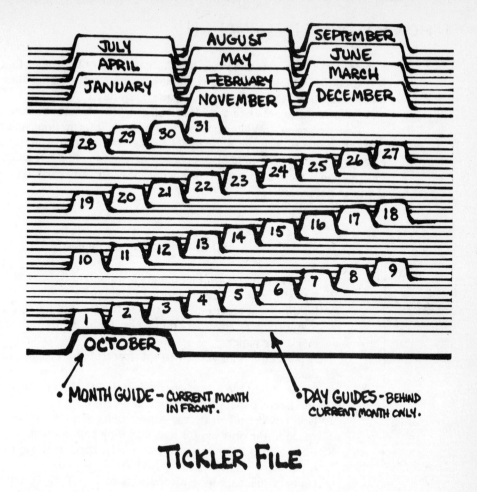

TICKLER FILE

One item they always saved was the minutes of a particular weekly meeting. I asked how many of them filed the minutes. All twenty-five members of the department raised their hands! That's twenty-four pieces of paper too many which had been filed away. Multiply twenty-four pieces of paper times each week of the year the meeting was held, and that's 1,200 unnecessary pieces of paper.

Those 1,200 worthless pieces of paper cost time, space, and money to save. Avoid the pack rat syndrome in your company. Locate *one* person in your department who is an incurable pack rat and appoint that person to save information. That person will love it, and you'll save time and paper. Be sure to have your department pack rat read the following section so he or she will be able to easily locate information again.

HOW TO LOCATE INFORMATION

Make an index. An index is an alphabetical list of the topics that you have filed. It is used like a table of contents. Having such an index makes it easy for others to find information in your files should you be absent.

An index also acts like a guide for others who file information for you.

Cross-reference. When an *important* piece of information can logically fit under more than one title in the file cabinet, make a note on the copies as to where the original is filed. On the note also include where supporting references and additional information is filed. Use cross-referencing sparingly, however. It can get out of hand if you're not careful.

MORE TIPS FOR EASY FILING

1. File as you go. Don't let papers accumulate to be filed later.
2. Use stiff guides for separation of categories.
3. Put the most recent information in the *front* of file folders.
4. Staple papers together, don't clip them. Clips only fall off or tangle the paper.
5. Attach copies of replies to the front of the original correspondence.
6. Neatly align the edges of papers you file. It takes just a second and keeps papers from getting dog-eared.
7. Don't overstuff drawers. Allow yourself four to five inches of space in the drawers for easy handling and looking.
8. File correspondence by subject, not by the date it was received or processed.
9. Consult the corporate attorney as to how long certain types of information must be kept. Weed out your files accordingly.
10. File individual names with last names first.
11. Avoid too big a miscellaneous file. When you accumulate five to ten pieces of paper in this file, make another file category for the information.
12. Lightly pencil in throw-away dates on filed material.
13. Fold oversized pieces of paper with the printing on the outside for quick reading.
14. If papers are removed from the file for any reason, put an OUT card in the file showing who has the material and the date it was taken.
15. To increase your filing speed, learn the alphabet backwards as well as frontwards. This way you don't have to say the alphabet each time to find a letter.
16. Have a place for everything. Don't leave paper lying around randomly. Don't pile. File.

USE G.U.T.S.

Imagine that there is a thin thread, a string, a thick rope, or a chain connecting you to every item and possession in your office. Do you feel entangled? Are you energized or drained by your attachments? Now visualize cutting yourself free from those unimportant papers, objects, and possessions. Lighten up by applying the G.U.T.S. method advocated by educator Charles Riley:

G = Give it away.

U = Use it.

T = Throw it away.

S = Sell it.

HARVEST TIME ON THE PAPER FARM

1. Make a map of everything that you have put out of sight. Keep the map handy for easy reference.
2. Begin a dump drawer.
3. Develop a parking system for everything that comes into your office.
4. When in doubt, throw it out.
5. Plan a trivia session.
6. Dump it.
7. Delay it.
8. Delegate it.
9. Do it.
10. Telephone when appropriate.
11. Agree on what to file. Don't keep everything.
12. Save warm-up time. Handle each piece of paperwork once.
13. Don't ask for it.
14. Answer correspondence briefly.
15. Streamline your files.
16. Set time limits on keeping information in your files.
17. Use topic files.
18. Make a tickler file.
19. Set up an important person or frequently called person file.
20. Give it away.
21. Use it.
22. Throw it away.
23. Sell it.

Since you spend so much time in your office, it's important that it be as pleasant as possible to assure your highest energy level, motivation, and on-the-job performance.

Layout
1. Rearrange the desk so it doesn't invite interruptions. Turn it away from the door and the water cooler so you aren't distracted by people walking by.
2. If it isn't possible to face away from people, put up a partition or place a bushy plant strategically between yourself and passersby.

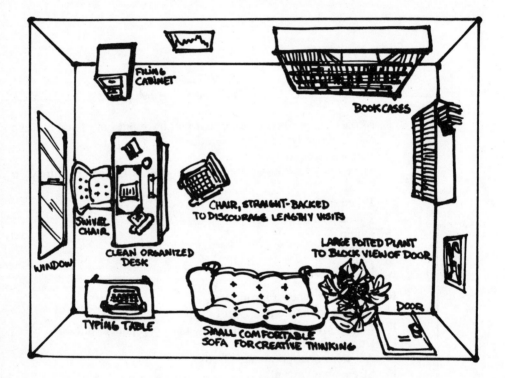

3. Arrange filing cabinets so they are within easy reach of your desk.
4. You may want a small sofa for creative thinking and short rest breaks; be sure it is not in sight of the door.

Colors
1. When decorating your office, use warm tones such as peach and pink to stimulate creativity, and green, blue-green, and blue to enhance concentration.

2. Avoid colors such as lavenders, cool yellows, and yellow-greens; they tend to give one's complexion a sallow look.

Lighting
1. Don't work facing a window. Make sure your light source comes from behind you and over your shoulder if you don't have ceiling lights.
2. Make sure your chair is comfortable. A swivel chair will enable you to do an about-face for a short look away from your work to rest your eyes.
3. If you've been doing close work for a while, look out a window for a vision break.
4. You might want to consider regular lighting rather than fluorescent lights; fluorescent lights can cause eyestrain and headaches in some people.

WORKING AT HOME

A fourteen-pound cat sleeps on Mr. Work-at-Home's desk. Important papers are filed in a bread box. At any time, Mr. W. can escape into the living room to lose himself in a game on his home video set, or wander into the kitchen for a snack. No business clients ever drop by, so he lets his "office" get cluttered. Repair people, landscapers, and Avon ladies call on him. He works out of his home and faces many of the same time challenges as people who take their work home from the office evenings and weekends. Here are several guidelines you can follow to make your "home work" easier.

Don't mix business and pleasure. Set aside a separate space for an office. It might be a spare bedroom, a dining room that can be closed off, or an area in the basement or attic. If you don't have a detached room, invest in partitions to separate yourself psychologically from the rest of the house. When you designate divisions between your work and your personal life, you can give more focused attention to each.

To further make the distinction between business and home life, "dress" for work. Don't sit around in your bathrobe all day. Consider "walking to work." Walk around the block and back to the house. This way, you get a little morning exercise and you arrive at your "office" in a more businesslike frame of mind, refreshed and ready for work. When you have meals or breaks, leave your work area; don't eat at your desk.

Organize your office space. Sure, no one sees your office, but clutter draws on your energy. Throw out the dead plants, close the closet doors, banish the cat from your desk, invest in some sturdy file cabinets, throw out empty boxes, and prioritize your reading and paperwork into "dump, delay, and do" categories.

Be firm with people who interrupt. Because you're working at home, others may not take your work as seriously as when you go to the office downtown. When you're at home, others may think you're more available to them: "Since you're right here anyway, could you mow the lawn after lunch or maybe fix the washer when you're ready to take a break?" Handle interruptions as you would in the office. Tell others when you'll be free. Hang a "quiet hour" or "do not disturb" sign on your door. Be assertive. Ask others to answer the doorbell when it rings. Use an answering machine to monitor incoming calls; you hear who's leaving the message and can decide whether or not to talk to the caller. If friends call during your work periods, resist the temptation to socialize. Have them call back later when it's more convenient for you.

Take yourself away from all this. If you work out of your home all the time, your life can get pretty insular. Go out for lunch or for a walk during your break. Getting out for a while helps keep your head clear, your thoughts fresh, and your energy high.

Your Action Plan

A. Clean and organize your desk according to the guidelines in this chapter.
B. Begin a dump drawer.
C. Develop a parking system for everything that comes into your office.
D. Streamline your files.
E. To get a big picture of your commitments, buy a monthly calendar-at-a-glance; avoid flipping through daily calendar pages.

Reminder: Are you continuing to break that bad time-management habit you vowed to eliminate in Chapter 2?

QUOTES TO CONSIDER

"Next to the dog, the wastebasket is man's best friend."
—B. C. Forbes

"Time is the scarcest resource and unless it is managed nothing else can be managed."
—Peter Drucker

"What a folly to dread the thought of throwing away life at once, and yet to have no regard to throwing it away by parcels and piecemeal."
—John Howe

6

THE PROGRAM EVALUATION AND REVIEW TECHNIQUE (PERT)

OBJECTIVES

When you finish this chapter, you will be able to:

- Design a PERT flow chart for all aspects of your job
- Visualize how your responsibilities contribute to your over-all professional objectives
- Use PERT to plan your next important project

What do rockets, spaghetti dinners, surprise parties, and your job all have in common? You can plan each of them by using the *program evaluation and review technique*. PERT is a flow chart that helps you clarify the directions in which your projects need to go. It includes all the steps and details that lead to the accomplishment of those directives.

PROJECT PLANNING

PERT is a valuable tool for:

1. Planning any project where graphic portrayal is needed to show relationships among various activities;
2. Visualizing a project for yourself or communicating it to others;
3. Keeping track of large projects;
4. Reducing projects into managable steps;
5. Troubleshooting.

OUTLINE YOUR PROFESSIONAL RESPONSIBILITIES

PERT helped me greatly when I was helping to design the fuel system for the Apollo moon rocket. The project manager kept assigning me more and more to do. It was getting out of hand. Finally, I made a diagram of everything I was already doing and gave it to him. As a result of my diagram, he realized how much he had been asking of me and he assigned two or three of the projects to other departments. Then he hired an assistant for me.

Following, you will find two PERT flow charts outlining the critical path method for giving a surprise party and for cooking a spaghetti dinner. If you cook like I do, open the wine first.

"THE SURPRISE PARTY"

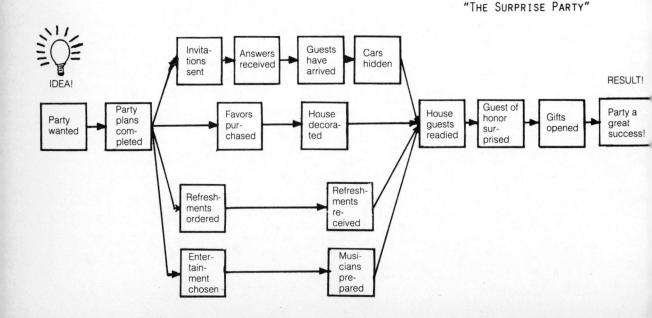

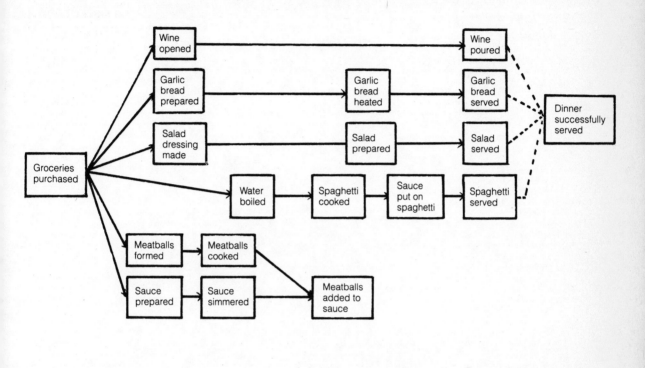

Your Action Plan

A. In the space provided, draw a PERT flow chart for your job. Include all the details for which you are responsible. When it comes time for a raise, take your PERT diagram in for your boss to see how busy you've been.

B. Create a PERT diagram for an upcoming project. List the milestones to be accomplished to complete the project. Show these events in a logical sequence. Connect them with lines to illustrate how one event leads to another. If activities can be done at the same time (either by yourself or by a number of co-workers), show this on a parallel path.

PERT Diagram for Your Job

**JOB
BEGUN**

**JOB OBJECTIVE
COMPLETED**

FLOW OF SUBTASKS TO COMPLETE OBJECTIVE

_____ QUOTE TO CONSIDER _____

"A straight path never leads anywhere except to the objective."
—André Gide

7

INTERRUP . . . TIONS

OBJECTIVES

When you finish this chapter, you will be able to:

- Spot the many ways you interrupt yourself
- Deal more effectively with interruptions from clients, customers, and other drop-in visitors
- Reduce the length of over-stays from subordinates, friends, and co-workers
- Handle interruptions from the boss more tactfully
- Implement a quiet hour

Are you one of those unfortunate people who gets interrupted during your interruptions? A person's average uninterrupted time at work is *less than ten minutes!* Imagine how much work you could do if you had large blocks of uninterrupted time.

SELF-INTERRUPTIONS

Do you interrupt yourself?

	YES	NO
1. Do you clutter your desk?	——	——
2. Do you ever take extended coffee or lunch breaks?	——	——
3. Do you procrastinate?	——	——
4. During the day, do you stop to say "hello" or to chat with co-workers?	——	——
5. Do you read tempting material when you should be working?	——	——
6. Does your mind wander throughout the day?	——	——
7. Do you make personal calls on office time?	——	——

If you answered "Yes" to *one or more* of the above questions, you are guilty of interrupting yourself. Be aware of how often you break the flow of your own thoughts and hinder your own progress on the job. Notice that when you point a finger at others to accuse them of interrupting you, three fingers point back at yourself!

IS THE APPOINTMENT REALLY NECESSARY?

Many appointments can be handled over the telephone. Before you agree to meet with someone, determine if the other person wants to give you information or to get information from you. In many cases, this can be accomplished with a phone call.

CLIENTS AND CUSTOMERS

If a client or a customer needs help with a problem, be certain that you are the right person to help. If you are, when you make the appointment, ask the client or the cutomer to be prepared with questions, solutions, and other pertinent information.

Control interruptions from clients simply by making appointments to see them. However, given human nature, emergencies may arise, people may be late, may miss appointments, or may hang around too long. Deal with occasional emergencies according to the dictates of the situation. If a client or customer is late, you may want to see him or her for a shorter period of time or make another appointment. People will respect your time if you demonstrate that *you* respect it. When the allotted time for the appointment is over, stand up and see the client or the customer to the door.

SUBORDINATES

Arrange regular staff meetings to deal with company business. At your convenience, set up conferences for individuals to ask work-related questions. Have them accumulate their questions for this period so they are not trailing in at all hours during the day and interrupting you. Be clear which employees are responsible directly to you; someone else may be able to help them more effectively.

THE BOSS

Often your job exists to support your boss. When it comes to setting priorities, your boss has the right-of-way. The key to dealing with your boss is to *communicate*. Arrange a short meeting in the mornings with your boss to align priorities. If it looks like you will have too much work, respond honestly. You might say something like, "Last month it took me two hours to prepare that report; I need the same amount of time this month, too." If you will have extra time during the day, suggest that you begin work early on an upcoming project. This encourages your boss to plan ahead. It may be helpful to share your time log or your PERT flow chart with your boss to help her or him better visualize how you spend your time.

During your short morning meeting, reinforce your boss's past good time management. For example, "I appreciated having the work ahead of time; I did a better job because I was not rushed." Communicate to your boss what you will be doing throughout the day so she or he will know what to expect from you in the way of production and will not overload you.

CO-WORKERS

People interrupt you for many reasons. Much of the time they need information, but just as often, their interruptions are not work-related at all. Some may be procrastinating on their own work. Others may want to visit. Still others will stop by to admire what a great job you're doing. Then there are those who just need a break.

Deal honestly with casual drop-ins. Tell them directly that you are busy. Suggest a better time to visit. Ultimately, they will respect you if they know what their limits are where your time is concerned.

HIDE OUT!

Go to a conference room, a library, or even to the lounge in the restroom for some quiet time. One manager I know sits in his car in the parking lot and gets a great deal of work done there. A harried college student who had to study for an important exam checked into a motel in another city for two days. She took all her books and notes along and found refuge in the fact that no one knew where she was and that her room didn't have a telephone. Many people go to work earlier and get ahead by putting in an hour of quality time before the office doors swing open for business.

Other people stay after hours. Still others find that it works well for them to take their lunch hours early and to work undisturbed while everyone else is at lunch.

SH-H-H! QUIET HOUR!

Quiet hour is a designated amount of time each day during which employees agree not to interrupt each other. This hour or so allows people crucial quality time to get their work done. Having a system of signals is one way of making quiet hour work. For example, after attending one of my time-management seminars, employees from one company put out small colored flags on their desks. A red flag, most often seen during quiet hours, signals, "Don't bother me unless it is an absolute emergency!" A green flag means, "Come in if you really need to." An orange or yellow flag means, "Caution. Come in, but it had better be important."

Inform people who normally interrupt you that you are working on a system to give you uninterrupted work time. Give them a definite time during which you do not want to be disturbed. Stick to that time faithfully every day so they will become accustomed to it. Minimize occasional interruptions by explaining firmly and politely to people who call or drop in exactly what you are doing. Tell them that you will call back when your quiet hour is over. You will then be able to return to your quality thinking without their problems and needs distracting you. Your quiet hour will pay off many times over.

Communicate the seriousness of your intentions from the very beginning. Co-workers may try to undermine your system. Some may be jealous. Others may be testing you to see if you mean what you say. Be prepared for this. Continue to be firm and consistent.

YOUR DESK OR MINE?

Meet people at *their* desks when you need something from them. By doing this, you are in control of the visit. Also, they have the information you need right at their fingertips. Be absolutely certain, however, that your business is important enough for you to be interrupting them.

REDUCE PERSONAL CONTACT WHILE WORKING

In our culture, there is an unwritten rule that eye contact invites small talk. Reduce interruptions by keeping your door shut or by strategically placing a bushy plant between you and people who can make eye contact. Arrange the angle of your desk so that you aren't looking up into the faces of passersby.

When walking down the hall, walk briskly with a purpose. If you saunter around, people will be more apt to stop you to talk. Do the following experiment. The next few times you have to walk somewhere, walk first with a determined look, eyes straight ahead. Then saunter, looking about you as you go. Count how many times you are interrupted during each of your walks and compare your results.

Don't be afraid that people might think that you are unfriendly if you minimize personal contact during working hours. Explain to them what you are accomplishing. You may discover that these tactics allow you to be even *more* friendly when it counts, during breaks, at lunch, after work. Because you have managed your time wisely, you will be more relaxed during your free time and more fun-loving. Because you've been assertive, you won't spend social time resenting those people who have interrupted you.

DEVELOP SIGNALS

A busy company president whom I know often gets cornered by talkative people. He has devised a signal with a couple of his assistants. When they see him nonchalantly rub his earlobe, they know that he wants them to come and rescue him by telling him that he is needed urgently somewhere. This never fails.

NO, NO, A THOUSAND TIMES NO!

If you're serious about reducing interruptions, learn to assert yourself. If you have trouble saying *no,* examine your reluctance. Are you afraid that you might let someone down when he or she needs your help? Are you worried that they won't like you if you refuse to drop everything and pay attention to them? Are you concerned that they won't help the next time *you* need help? You must be protective of your valuable time! Exaggerate this protectiveness until it becomes natural. People will admire you for your firm stand.

STAND UP TO INTERRUPTIONS

If you have unexpected visitors, stand up when they come into the room. It's a rare person who is going to plop down in a chair in your office while you are still standing. To further protect yourself, don't even keep a chair near your desk.

Your Action Plan

A. List the ways you interrupt yourself. How will you do things differently from now on?
B. List the kinds of interruptions you get from others. How are you going to handle these from now on?
C. Implement a daily quiet hour for yourself, your department, or your company. Decide when it will start, how long it will last, and what signals you will use to indicate when it is in effect.
D. Schedule a specific time each day to meet with people. Encourage others to make their appointments with you during that time.
E. Get rid of the extra chair in your office, or leave a notebook lying on it so that people will stay only if you invite them.
F. Come to the office earlier, stay later, or work through your lunch hour and eat earlier or later.

QUOTE TO CONSIDER

"How sweet, how passing sweet, is solitude!"
—William Cowper

8

TELEPHONE HANG-UPS

When you finish this chapter, you will be able to:

- Reduce your telephone time at least 25 percent
- Implement a successful call-back system
- Avoid losing at the game of telephone tag
- Let telephone technology save you time
- Avoid being put on hold when you call long distance
- Get others to return your calls without procrastinating
- Cut off long-winded talkers without offending them
- Keep a telephone log
- Put sparkle in your telephone conversations

Is the telephone your master or your servant?

In surveys that I have conducted, I've found that 90 percent of executives usually spend *over an hour a day* on the telephone. Over 40 percent of executives often spend *two hours or more a day* on the phone. If you read and apply the ideas in this chapter, you will probably reduce your telephone time 25–50 percent, and still be just as effective on the phone.

OVERCOME THE NEUROTIC NEED TO ANSWER THE TELEPHONE

Most people have a compulsion to answer a ringing phone, whether from curiosity or from the fear of loss. Are *you* so addicted? Test yourself the next time the phone rings. Don't answer it, or think back to a time when you couldn't answer a ringing phone for some reason. Then answer the following questions.

1. When the phone first started ringing, did your body automatically jump to answer it?

YES_____ NO_____

2. What happened to your concentration on your work?

_____

_____

3. As the phone continued to ring, did you feel exceedingly nervous?

YES_____ NO_____

4. When it stopped ringing, did you feel regret, disappointment, or fear that you might have missed something important?

YES_____ NO_____

Answering the telephone may be an integral part of your job if you are in sales or similar professions. However, it is wise for most people to detoxify themselves from the need to answer the phone every time it rings, or on the first ring. Without such dependence, you can continue working if you are in the middle of something important, or you can take a few seconds longer to make note of what you have been doing. After the call, you can return to your work more easily.

HOW TO USE TELEPHONE NEUROSIS TO YOUR ADVANTAGE

A favorite story of mine is about the time the ambassador from England was visiting with President Franklin D. Roosevelt. The President kept getting telephone calls. During one of these interruptions, the ambassador left the Oval Office, found a telephone outside, waited a short while, then called the President. When the President answered, the ambassador requested his undivided attention, which he was promptly granted.

More than once, I've been in hotels with long lines at the front desk when I've been in a hurry and had questions. In cases like this, I go to the nearest telephone and call the desk. Someone always answers immediately because of their compulsion to pick up a ringing phone, and I am helped right away. This strategy also works when counters at airlines are busy and a person has to change reservations in a hurry.

THE ROTATION SYSTEM

If you work in an office and don't have anyone to answer the phone, arrange with co-workers to sign up for certain hours during which one of you will answer the phone for everyone. This gives everyone a bit of protected time.

STAY OUT OF THE WIND

While the telephone is a remarkable invention that enables us to save enormous amounts of time, it is also one of the most ingenious ways for people to interrupt us. Many people who would not think of interrupting us when we are concentrating on our work think nothing of calling when we are in the middle of something. Since they can't see us, they feel absolved from the guilt of knowing that they have intruded. Keep these interruptions as brief as possible.

Answer the phone, "Hello, XYZ Company, John Smith speaking, how may I help you?" This encourages specific answers from callers who might otherwise be long-winded if asked an open-ended question. An example of an open-ended questions would be, "Hi, Bob, how are you?" This invites Bob to supply you with a detailed account of everything from his most recent travels to a progress report on his health.

Have you ever noticed that when people call you from out of town often the first thing they want is a weather report? How often have *you* given them a weather report and asked for theirs in exchange? If neither of you is going to visit the other, what difference does it make what the weather is? If you feel obliged to give a weather report, at least keep it brief. You don't have to go into relative humidity and cold front information! Sometimes this seemingly meaningless socializing is a way to "grease the rails" into the real conversation. Be sensitive to this; play the game if you must, but don't let it play you.

When you call someone, know ahead of time what you are going to say, and get right to the point. For example, say, "Hi, Betty. I'm calling about three changes in your order." This businesslike approach keeps the conversation from meandering.

When callers want to talk on and on, tell them tactfully that you are too busy to visit and suggest a better time for them to call. Signal the end of a conversation by saying something like, "Just one more thing, Dan, before we hang up . . ."

One executive was telling me his technique for reducing the time he spends on the telephone. He answers the phone, *"Go!"* and if the caller doesn't talk fast, he hangs up! Thinking that he had gotten a little carried away with trying to save time, I asked how this strategy was working for him. He replied that very few people call him anymore!

WILL YOU HOLD?

Being put on hold seems to be a fact of life these days. If you are calling long distance and are asked to hold, you can state that you are calling long distance and prefer not to wait. It's worth a try. Or you might inquire how long the person with whom you wish to speak will be on the other line, in the meeting, or whatever. Ask the secretary to slip the other person a note indicating that you are on hold.

Some answering services and secretaries, however, don't give callers a chance. They answer, "Hello, ABC Company, please hold." And there you are, stuck on hold for who knows how long. When this happens to Mary L., a financial analyst, she holds for a minute if she's calling long distance. Then she hangs up, calls later, and before the person who answers can say a word, Mary announces that she's calling long distance and does not want to be put on hold while the other person answers more incoming calls and handles other business. This approach gives Mary a fighting chance.

DIRTY TRICKS

Honesty *is* the best policy. Being up front with people and telling it like it is will usually help you handle the most difficult telephone situations. However, over the years, people have shared with me all kinds of devious little tricks for getting through to busy people and for ending telephone conversations or ending conversations they'd rather not be having in the first place. I don't recommend that *you* use these techniques. Just be aware that they might be used by others and may consequently interfere with you getting you job done.

Getting Through to Busy People

1. Ask for them by their first names or nicknames; if questioned as to what your call is regarding, reply that it's personal.
2. Tell their secretaries that the call is about the $300 that they owe you; most people will come on the line immediately to contest the fact that they owe anyone money.
3. Avoid secretaries who screen calls by telephoning before or after hours. Busy executives often come in early or stay late, and when the phone rings, they're likely to answer it out of curiosity.
4. Call the president's office first. When they refer you to the proper department, you can then call and state that the president's office referred you. Your call may be given higher priority this way than if it just came in cold.

Cutting Phone Conversations Short

1. Knock loudly on your desk and say that you have to hang up, there's someone at your door.
2. Have a tape recording of a phone ringing. Play it when callers get long-winded and tell them you have another call.
3. Tell the caller that you can hardly hear him or her; you must have a bad connection. Then hang up in the middle of *your* sentence. No one would ever believe that you'd hang up on yourself while you were talking. Leave the phone off the hook for a few minutes in case he or she tries to call back.
4. To avoid talking with people all together, call them during their lunch hours or breaks when you're sure they'll be out.

AVOID TELEPHONE TAG

Let's say that you call Joe and he's in a meeting. He returns your call and discovers that you've gone to lunch early. You call back in the afternoon, but he's on break. You and Joe are victims of a frustrating phenomena called *telephone tag*. A good call-back system will help reduce such wasted time.

1. Have someone answer your phone at least part of the day and get the names and numbers of callers and why they called. The person who answered the phone might be able to help them better than you or refer them to someone else who can. Have the person who answers find out the best time for you to return their calls. When you have all this information, you can better prepare for your calls, have the necessary information handy, and reduce your chances of missing the other parties.
2. If people call during your quiet hour, have your secretary tell them that you are in a meeting. They don't have to know that it's with yourself!
3. Give your secretary an exact script to follow that outlines how you want callers handled. Prepare a *hit list* of people with whom you do not want to speak. It's imperative, however, that your secretary recognize their voices and tell them that you are busy *before* they give their names (Have you ever given someone else's secretary *your* name and *then* been told that the other person just stepped out? It makes you wonder if that person would have been in if you'd been someone else). By the same token, prepare a VIP list of people for your secretary to put through to you immediately.
4. Set time limits for others to return your calls. If you ask people to call back as early as possible or at their convenience, that could be any time. Instead, ask them to call back by a certain date and time.
5. Don't feel that you have to keep returning someone's call who is constantly out. Nick G., a general manager for a social services agency, returns all calls he receives. If people are not in, he crumples up their numbers and throws them away. He rationalizes with a grin, "They need *me*, I don't need them! They'll call again if it's really important." This way, he very successfully avoids playing telephone tag.

THE VALUE OF KEEPING A TELEPHONE LOG

A telephone log provides you with a permanent record of all your important phone calls. It documents dates, people called, subjects covered, and decisions made. It helps you organize your thoughts before making calls and record the outcome of those calls.

To start your log, write the following across the top of a piece of notebook paper:

Date	Name	#	Points to Cover	Actions/Decisions

Whenever you have something to say to someone, write it down under points to cover. If possible, wait until you have several topics to discuss and cover them in one call. This will keep you from scattering your energy with several calls. When you reach the other person, check off the points as you cover them. Jot down the date you made the call. Make notes of the actions required or of the decisions made. If you are unable to reach the other parties, when they return your call you'll be able to look up quickly what you wanted to discuss with them.

With these comments, I'm going to hang up this chapter.

HOW TO PUT SPARKLE INTO YOUR PHONE CONVERSATIONS

1. Be dynamic. Avoid long pauses and nonwords such as *ahhhh* and *ummmm*. Have a list of the topics you want to cover right beside you so you don't have to search your memory for what you wanted to say.
2. Set a time limit on your calls so you can get right to the point. Time yourself with a stopwatch or an egg timer.
3. Smile into a mirror while talking on the phone to put more life into your voice.
4. Get more enthusiasm into those calls by standing up and gesturing while you speak.
5. Tape yourself and study your voice. Is it interesting, pleasant, full of enthusiasm? Does it have enough inflection? Practice with a tape recorder until you are satisfied that your voice is interesting and authoritative enough to command the attention of others.

Your Action Plan

A. Inform everyone who calls you from now on as to the best time to reach you. Try to make it the same time period each day so you can group your telephone interruptions.
B. Place an egg timer or stopwatch by your telephone. Try to limit your calls to three minutes.
C. Prepare a hit list for your secretary. You might want to put it in code so no one else reads it.
D. Begin a telephone log.
E. Set up a call-back system.
F. Make a recording of your voice. Practice ways to make it authoritative and interesting.

QUOTE TO CONSIDER

"In heaven when the blessed use the telephone they will say what they have to say and not a word besides."

—Somerset Maugham

9

STOP PROCRASTINATING!

When you finish this chapter, you will be able to:

- Understand why people procrastinate
- State your desired goals clearly in written form
- Use the salami method to break goals into smaller, less threatening steps
- Build motivation for projects
- Develop commitment for a job
- Follow through on projects
- Work to natural stopping places for a sense of completion

Think of something that you have been putting off starting. Is it *worth* doing? If so, why haven't you already done it? The excuses I get from clients generally go like this: "I haven't had the time." "I don't know where to start." "It's too big a job." "I've had other priorities."

When we look beneath the surface, we discover several reasons why they *really* haven't done the job.

1. *Lack of a deadline.* Without setting deadlines, we don't get serious about getting something done. After all, we can't be late doing something if we haven't set a deadline.
2. *The deadline is too far away.* How often have you waited until the last minute to start something and then had a frantic finish? For example, have you ever waited until the last minute to organize your income tax, or waited until the night before to cram for an exam the next day? Some people claim to work better under pressure, but it's a dangerous habit to develop. Too many things can go wrong and throw your timing off. You also pay a high price for mental wear and tear.
3. *Fear of failure or other consequences.* If you don't try, you won't fail. But then again, you won't succeed, either. Some people don't finish their projects because they fear the consequence of *succeeding* and the additional responsibilities it brings. For example, if you succeed in increasing your income significantly, it would be to your advantage to learn how to invest it wisely. Investing, if you are not familiar with it, is a whole new area of study.
4. *The snowball effect.* Procrastination often begins with you not doing some little thing because the time isn't right or you don't feel like doing it. Something else comes along that you don't feel like doing, and you postpone that, too. Now you have two things that by themselves appear small, but together they might be enough to create an area of resistance within you against finishing either of them. After a while, three or four or five items have piled up and procrastination is rampant. There are so many things for you to do, you might feel overwhelmed by the thought of even starting. You might do anything to avoid the moment of truth.
5. *Lack of motivation.* This is the underlying cause of most procrastination. To discover if this is the reason behind your procrastinating, ask yourself, "If someone held a gun to my head and told me to get this project done by the deadline *or else.* . . .could I do it?" If the answer is *yes,* continue with the following.

1. *Put your goal in writing:* Ask yourself exactly what it is that you want to accomplish. Don't confuse the task with the objective. For example, a task is cleaning your desk, but the *objective* is to work at a clean, organized workspace.

When you write your goal, focus on the results, not on the process.

DON'T WRITE:	BUT RATHER WRITE:
"I'm going to start painting my house."	"My house is painted by April 3."
"I'm going to lose weight."	"I weigh my perfect weight by September 15."
"I'm going to ask for a raise."	"Raise granted, January 1."

GOAL_____

2. *Build motivation for the project.* Instead of seeing yourself slaving over a difficult project, imagine how finishing the job will enhance your career. For example, rather than focusing on how difficult it will be to reorganize your filing system, think about all the time and energy you'll save when it's done.

The key is to *want to do the things that you have to do.* What other choice is there? You can do things and resent them, or do things to your advantage with enthusiasm because you can clearly see the gains you receive from doing them.

A. Make a list of all the benefits that you will enjoy for having achieved your goal.

BENEFIT_____

_____

BENEFIT_____

_____

BENEFIT_____

_____

BENEFIT_____

_____

B. Make a list of the consequences of not achieving your goal.

CONSEQUENCE_____

_____

CONSEQUENCE_____

_____

CONSEQUENCE_____

_____

3. *Use the salami method to achieve your goal.* If your project is worth doing at all, it is worth doing a piece at a time in order to be done well. You wouldn't eat a salami whole. You'd cut it into slices. Do the same thing to consume your project. Divide it into steps. For example, if you have a lengthy report to prepare, you might divide the project in the following way: experts consulted; data gathered; report written; report revised; report typed; report duplicated; final report distributed. After each step, assign a deadline. Now, instead of having one gigantic report to finish, you have a series of less threatening, smaller steps, each with its own deadline.

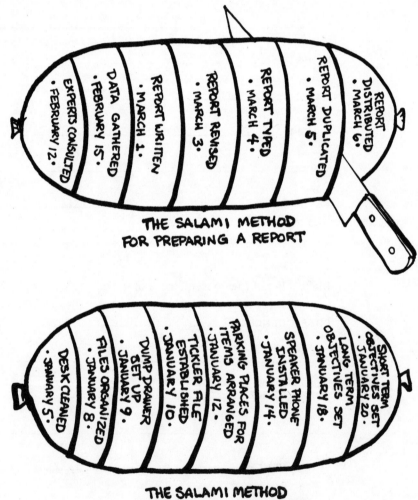

THE SALAMI METHOD
FOR PREPARING A REPORT

THE SALAMI METHOD
FOR GETTING ORGANIZED

4. G.O.Y.A. *(Get off your . . . anatomy).* In Texas, they tell the story of a dog that used to sit every day on the same patch of ground. One day, a cactus started growing where the dog liked to sit. The dog sat right down anyway, and it howled and howled. Every day it went back to the same spot to sit and howl. Why didn't he move? Like so many people you might know, it would rather howl than change where it was used to sitting.

How can you overcome procrastination? Why, just get off your cactus . . . or shall we wait until later?

1. Tell yourself that you'll work on the project *just 10 minutes*. After that, you may have begun a momentum and won't want to stop. If you do stop for some reason, you'll be 10 minutes closer to your goal.
2. Make it a game to finish in time.
3. Cut off your escapes. Put away tempting distractions. Hide magazines. Turn off the TV. Hang a conference sign on your door so you won't be disturbed. Pull the curtains so you can't gaze out the window.
4. Stay in the vicinity. For example, if you have to make a phone call, stay by the telephone.
5. Work to natural stopping places. You'll feel less scattered and more satisfied. For example, don't stop reading in the middle of a section. Finish fully. Read to the end of an article or chapter.
6. Use the buddy system. Make a commitment to your project by giving a copy of it and your respective deadlines to a colleague. Report regularly on your progress.
7. Start, no matter what, *start!* If you have a call to make, pick up the phone and start dialing. If you have a letter to write, put paper in the typewriter and start typing.

Your Action Plan

A. Pick a goal on which you've been procrastinating. List the benefits of doing the job and the consequences for not doing it. Make a salami of the job. Slice it into smaller pieces and assign deadlines to each step.
B. G.O.Y.A.

"You delay but time does not."

—Benjamin Franklin

"Even if you're on the right track, you'll get run over if you just sit there."

—Anonymous

"One of these days is none of these days."

—English proverb

10

SPEED-READING

When you finish this chapter, you will be able to:

- Apply basic speed-reading techniques to all your reading
- Test your comprehension
- Double your reading speed and improve your understanding
- Breeze through newspapers
- Reduce the habit of pronouncing the words by yourself when you read
- Read smarter by using seventeen proven techniques

Are you having trouble getting *out* of the in-basket at work? Would you like more time for pleasure reading? You can become a faster, more effective reader the minute you apply the following techniques.

PREVIEW BEFORE YOU READ

When we learn or perceive something, we usually go from the general to the specific. When you walk into a room, you see the entire room first, then begin to notice the details, the pattern in the carpet, the view from the windows, the design in the curtains. Likewise, you will be a better reader if you first obtain a preview of a section before you read, then read and relate the details to the overall theme. This strategy improves your comprehension and recall.

Take a moment now to practice this. Preview the rest of this chapter. With your hand in a relaxed position, sweep your hand down the middles of the pages.

Do not go all the way to either margin, but stop about one-quarter inch short of the print on each side.

SWEEPING PREVIEW HAND TECHNIQUE

Allow the movement of your hand to guide your eyes smoothly down the page. Do not force your eyes to follow your hand exactly, rather, let them drift back and forth down the pages looking for ideas. Remember, this is a *preview* technique, so you won't be reading *per se*.

Preview the rest of the chapter now. Then return to this point and continue reading.

PREVIEWING PRACTICE

For the next week, practice your previewing techniques every day. Select a fairly easy novel or two. Do not chose stories or technical material at first.

Since you are retraining your eyes and mind to read in a new way, make sure the print in your novel is easy on the eyes and not too small. Place a bookmark in the middle of your practice book and preview from the beginning of the book to the marker. Glance down blank pages as well so as not to break your rhythm.

When you reach the marker, return to the beginning. Glance through again, all the time questioning yourself: What's this book about? Who are the characters? What ideas can I pick up before going back and reading the material?

During these previewing drills, allow yourself about four or five seconds a page.

You may notice that when you first begin working with this technique, you see more words on either the right or the left pages, or on the tops or the bottoms of pages. At first, several whole pages may fly by without your noticing anything. Don't worry about this—it's perfectly normal while you are getting used to perceiving more rapidly. Throughout the week, continue to practice previewing. Even out your technique by noticing something in every paragraph. As you become more comfortable with your previewing techniques, you will start to relax and gain confidence. And you will pick up more and more information.

PACE YOURSELF AS YOU READ

After you've previewed a section of material or a chapter in your regular reading, brush along under the lines with your hand. This is a tighter technique than the sweeping previewing technique. Smoothly underline every sentence until you become comfortable with the technique, then speed up until you become comfortable with that. Eventually you will be moving quickly down the page, brushing under every three or four lines of print.

Brush to within one-quarter inch of the margins on each side. Use three fingers instead of one (if you point as you read, you may have a tendency to focus on one word at a time).

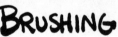

BRUSHING PRACTICE

As you continue to read this chapter and other books and reading material throughout the week, use the brushing technique. After a week or so of practicing each day, it is possible to double your reading rate. Pace yourself in all your reading after you have previewed a section, article, or chapter.

HOW TO REDUCE SUBVOCALIZATION

Pronouncing the words silently to yourself when you read is probably the habit that slows you down the most. Pick a short article and make a gentle humming sound to yourself as you pace yourself and read. The humming fills your mind with another sound and makes it harder for you to say the words to yourself. Eventually you'll begin to read silently through the humming. You will be reading by sight instead of by sound. Hum only during short practice periods. There's no need to hum all the time, especially if you are reading in public!

A second exercise to help you overcome subvocalization is to allow your eyes to drift down the center of a narrow newspaper column and pick up just the key ideas. You will find that, after a while, you'll begin to see and understand the connecting words without saying each one of them. Let your peripheral vision, the vision out of the corners of your eyes, pick up the words at the edges of the columns.

It may be difficult to eliminate subvocalization entirely. Even the best readers still subvocalize somewhat, but they've greatly reduced it. You can increase your reading rate significantly by merely subvocalizing the key words: names of people, places, things, and action words. You still see and understand the rest of the words, but you don't pronounce them.

Practice reading *very fast* on material for which you will not be held responsible. This way, you challenge yourself to go faster and faster without being afraid that you'll miss something important. And your regular work-related reading will be faster because you've practiced.

TWO HINTS FOR READING TECHNICAL MATERIAL

Technical material can be approached differently from stories and novels. You still preview and read with a purpose so that certain facts attract your attention. However, with technical reading, you can benefit greatly from *changing the order* of your reading.

Last things first. Always read summaries and conclusions first, then prefaces and introductions. Then glance through any charts, graphs, or pictures. This may be all you need to do to get what you want from the material. If you need to, then glance back through the main body of material for additional supporting evidence and examples.

Use checkpoints. With a soft-lead pencil, make checks in the margins next to unfamiliar words so you can look them up later if they're not explained in the text as you continue to read. Also mark passages you want to study more carefully later. When you've learned the material, you can easily erase the checks.

TEST YOUR COMPREHENSION

After you've read a section, set the material aside and think about it. You might want to go through the contents, index, or glossary and verbally review the ideas for yourself or for a friend. This is an excellent way to evaluate where your strengths and weaknesses are in remembering the material.

Ask yourself if you satisfied your purpose for reading the material. Did you read to be entertained, to gain information, to learn a new skill, or to improve yourself? Did you accomplish your purpose? If you did, then your comprehension was good.

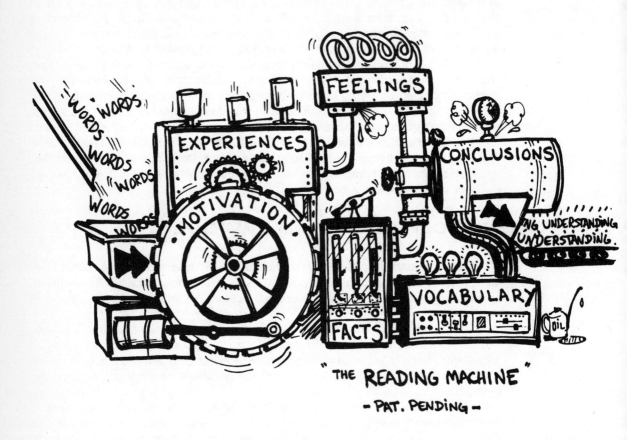

"THE READING MACHINE"
— PAT. PENDING —

You'll more fully understand what you've read if you do something with your new knowledge. For example, instead of just reading theories about how to organize your desk, apply what you've learned. This way, theories become reality and what you've read is more meaningful.

The ideas in this book come to life when you follow through. *Full speed ahead!*

MORE IDEAS FOR READING SMARTER

Maintain good posture. It's okay to read with your feet propped up on your desk, but don't expect to achieve your fastest reading rates in this position. Poor posture impedes circulation, and concentration drops. For best results, don't get too comfortable. It isn't necessary to sew thorns in your clothes like the ancient mystics did, but you should be sitting in a straight-backed chair at a desk or a table. Hold the book at about a forty-five-degree angle in front of you with all points equidistant from your eyes. This posture impresses on your mind that you mean business!

If you read while you're eating, realize that in doing so, you are dividing your attention between your food and the book. Your concentration will not be as good. If you read to fall asleep, you have three strikes against good concentration. First of all, when you're sitting in bed, your posture is not that good. Second, if it's a good book, you'll be torn between the desire to stay up and finish it and the need to go to sleep. Third, you run the risk of impressing on your mind that you sometimes use reading to fall asleep. The next day at the office, as you face a long report, this negative programming could interfere with your attention for the task at hand.

Keep a clean workspace. Piles of papers and books strewn about your office will only draw on your energy and dilute your full attention from your reading. Clean it up!

Set time limits on reading. Your reading expands or contracts to fill the time you allow for it. If it normally takes you all Monday morning to read a report, for example, next Monday challenge yourself to finish it by 10:30 A.M. Set natural time limits by finishing your reading *before* you have to be somewhere—before you go to lunch, before your next appointment, before you go home from work.

Read selectively. Ask yourself how reading a particular book, magazine, or newspaper contributes to your life. If it doesn't enrich you in some way such as entertaining you, informing you, or advancing your career, don't read it! There's so much material demanding our attention these days that we can't afford to read that which is irrelevant.

Limit your subscriptions to newspapers, journals, and magazines. If you try to read everything written on a subject, you'll discover that information begins to repeat itself. The same is true with reference materials. Purchase a few good, recent reference books on your topic and study those alone.

Know where the important information is. Remember, in technical reading and many nonfiction books, summaries and conclusions can tell the whole story. Read them first. If you still want supporting information, glance back through the text. Look for most of the key ideas in the first and last sentences of paragraphs.

Prioritize your reading. Just as you prioritize your mail, divide your reading into *dump, delegate, delay,* and *do* categories.

Dump: Into this category go all those newspapers, brochures, and low-priority mail you have been *intending* to read. Newspapers continue to print follow-up stories, so you won't be missing a great deal if you skip a few days. You can also count on receiving sales letters from the same people about three times before they figure you aren't interested. Look for bulk-

reading a book

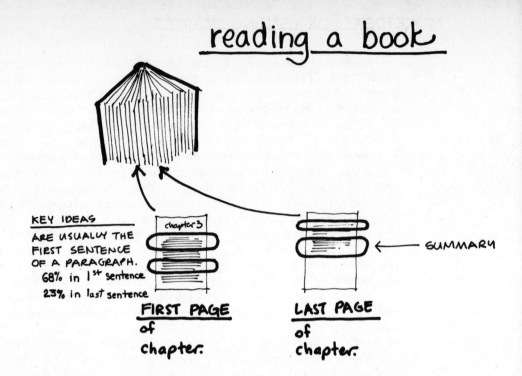

KEY IDEAS ARE USUALLY THE FIRST SENTENCE OF A PARAGRAPH. 68% in 1st sentence 23% in last sentence

chapter 3

FIRST PAGE of chapter.

LAST PAGE of chapter.

SUMMARY

rate mail from the same companies about six to ten times before they drop you. Catch these items on the third or fourth time around.

Delegate: Assign job-related periodicals to your staff members to read. At meetings, have each of them highlight relevant articles. In one company I know, a secretary photocopies the table of contents of trade journals and distributes them to everyone. People then *order* the articles they want to read. The secretary copies those articles and sends them out. This way, people aren't encumbered with articles that don't interest them.

Delay: Slip material that is not time-critical into your briefcase to read when you have some down time before appointments, when put on hold, or while waiting in a line.

Do: After you've done all of the above, start reading. Use the speed reading principles: preview the material first, then pace yourself with your hand motions as you read.

Target your reading. The next time you pick up a magazine, look at the contents page, decide which article is the most important for you to read, and begin there. Then, if you still have time, read the remaining articles in order of decreasing value to you.

News stories are constructed so that the important information is in the headline and the first few paragraphs. Read those and skim the rest if you don't have time to read everything. Feature stories, on the other hand, often have more information as the story continues, so look for the gist of the article further into the story.

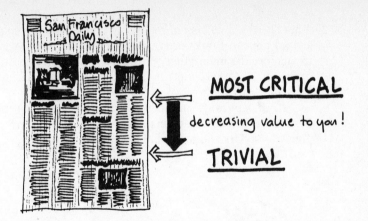

Make appointments to do your reading. You are every bit as important as your clients, and no good to them if you feel tired and overwhelmed with reading. Pencil yourself in on your datebook every day, every other day, or once a week, and keep your appointment with yourself to do your reading.

Swap reading. Staying current in today's world takes a lot of time. Have associates read certain articles or journals and you agree to read others. Lunch together regularly and exchange information.

Tear out articles you come across that would interest your associate. This way, they don't have to cover everything written in the field. Ask them to do the same for you, and you have multiplied yourself.

Choose steaks, not stacks. Take a professional to dinner and inquire about the state of the art. Have your professional recommend the most timely articles in your field of interest. You may find that two hours over steaks can be more fun than the same amount of time spent in the dark, lonesome library stacks.

Get good value out of your reading time. Decide how thoroughly you really have to read. If you're reading highly technical material for details, read more slowly. If you just want an overview, glance quickly through the material.

Manage by exception. Do you receive regular reports that you could reduce in frequency? For example, if you receive a weekly report on absenteeism in your department, could you ask for it only when absenteeism rises above a certain percentage? This can reduce your reading load.

Don't get on mailing lists. They've finally discovered something that multiplies faster than rabbits: mailing lists. Whenever you sign your name and address, you will most likely appear on multiple mailing lists. If you sign, but don't wish to be on a list, indicate that beside your signature. Write to people who already have your name and ask to be removed from their lists. You also might want to contact the Direct Mail Marketing Association, headquartered in New York City (6 East 43rd Street, New York, NY 10017, [212] 689-4977). They can have your name removed from the mailing lists of a significant number of mail order companies.

Recognize that more can be less. Writers often have very good ideas, but they don't always have *long* ideas. Many times, ominous-looking volumes are not as long as they appear. Books can be bulked in many ways: with extra examples and stories to support the main point (only read what you need to in order to understand the main point); larger print; more space between the lines; heavier paper. Don't be intimidated by *fat* books.

Read in bites. It's more encouraging to finish a section at a time than to try to get through an entire book in an undefined amount of time. Section a book into parts and give yourself a deadline to finish each section.

Cut through jargon. Business letters are often very formal or flowery. Cut through the jargon immediately to discover what the sender wants. For example: "We are in receipt of your contribution of November 5, 1983. Thank you for all your continued support. Please be assured that your gift is greatly appreciated." In other words, "Thank you for your contribution."

Subscribe to a clipping bureau. Clipping bureaus, listed in the Yellow Pages, are services that cover daily and weekly newspapers and consumer and trade magazines, looking for articles about the topics you specify. In addition to their initial charge, they ask a finder's fee per clipping. Indicate in your contract with them that you want *one* copy of each story, especially if it is carried in a syndicated column run in numerous newspapers. With a clipping bureau on your side, you can relax about missing something important in the news.

During a business meeting, do you miss important points because you are not taking notes fast enough? And do you have to ask people to repeat telephone messages because you cannot write as fast as callers speak? If so, you undoubtedly write in longhand.

You could, of course, overcome this waste of time by learning shorthand (there are more than two hundred copyrighted systems). Or you can take the world's fastest course in speed-writing, which is outlined here.

LEAVE OUT UNNECESSARY VOWELS AND CONSONANTS.
Lv out uncsry vwls & cnsnts.

ABBREVIATE WHENEVER POSSIBLE.
Abrev whn poss.

DEVELOP YOUR OWN SHORTCUTS.
Dvlp shrtcts.
(4 ex., see = c, you = u, easy = ez).

Now try these sentences & c hw u do:

YOU CAN WRITE FASTER IF YOU ABBREVIATE.

_____

THE BEST WAY TO LEARN SPEED-WRITING IS TO PRACTICE.

_____

SPEED-WRITING IS EASY AND SAVES TIME, TOO.

_____

SPEED-WRITING IS A BLESSING FOR POOR SPELLERS.

_____

CAN ANYONE READ WHAT YOU HAVE WRITTEN?

_____

Starting today, make the decision to write faster. Practice by taking notes at meetings and seminars. Take all your phone messages using your new skill. You may decide that you need two systems: one for your own use and another—also abbreviated, but containing a few more letters—for times when other people may have to see your notes.

You also might want to train your secretary and co-workers how to speed-write.

And now, as you read the next section of this book, take notes using speed-writing. Pass the notes along to someone else to read.

Your Action Plan

A. From now on, preview material before you read it. Then pace yourself as you read.
B. Apply at least four of the *reading smarter* strategies in the next week.
C. Turn to the contents in this book. Select the most important chapter for you to read next. Preview the chapter. Then read the section, using your pacing technique.

QUOTES TO CONSIDER

"The writer only begins a book. The reader finishes it."
—Goethe

"If you were to read one book a week for every week of your life, you would only have read one-tenth of one percent of all the books in the New York Public Library. The trick is to know which books to read."
—Carl Sagan

"We will find nothing in books which has no existence in ourselves.
—Robert Davies

"Knowledge is of two kinds: we know a subject ourselves or we know where we can find information about it."
—Samuel Johnson

"It is well to read everything of something, and something of everything.
—Henry Brougham

11

ZZZ SPEED-SLEEPING ZZZ

OBJECTIVES

When you finish this chapter and have practiced the exercises, you will be able to:

- Reduce the amount of time you need to sleep each night
- Practice speed-sleeping at both your office and at home
- Enjoy the benefits of two hours' sleep in as little as ten minutes of speed-sleeping
- Use speed-sleeping to reduce stress and to quickly relax
- Awaken regularly without an alarm clock
- Use speed-sleeping to help you to think more clearly

How can you put more time into your life? You can't! What you *can* do, however, is to have more *conscious* hours in your life. You can do this by learning to sleep less and by staying more alert while you are awake.

QUANTITY SLEEP VERSUS QUALITY SLEEP

Tonight, go to bed an hour later than you normally do and wake up tomorrow morning at your usual time.

What was your reaction to this suggestion? Did you react negatively? *"What? Go to bed an hour later than usual? Are you crazy? I have to work tomorrow. I'll be tired!"* How do you know that you'll be tired? It isn't even tomorrow yet!

If you resisted this suggestion, you may have accepted the common belief that the quantity of sleep we get affects how we feel the following morning. The truth, however, is that the *quality* of our sleep is what affects how we feel.

In school, I was told that people sleep one-third of their lives, which I computed to be eight hours of sleep each night. If I slept six hours, I expected to be "two hours tired" the next day. My parents reinforced this belief by often stating, "It's late; you'll be tired if you don't go to bed right now." My belief about needing a lot of sleep was a little like a nail people kept tapping. Eventually, after it had been tapped so many times, it became an embedded suggestion in my mind.

HOW TO IMPROVE THE QUALITY OF YOUR SLEEP

Two ways to improve the quality of your sleep are: 1) to eat right; and 2) to exercise regularly. Another way is to think positive thoughts as you drift off into sleep. This is the time when your mind is most suggestible. As an experiment, just before you go to sleep tonight, observe your thoughts. Do you mumble suggestions to yourself such as, "Oh, it's late, I'm going to be so tired tomorrow"? Or do you dwell on personal problems when it's late and you're all alone? Do you watch violent television shows before you turn in? Perhaps you listen to the late night news, which tells you of the most recent killings and burnings and robberies. Negative thinking before sleep tends to lower the quality of sleep. Pessimists often need more sleep than optimists. In fact, for many negative thinkers, the most pleasant thing they prefer to do is to stay unconscious for as long as possible!

Optimists, on the other hand, usually think positive thoughts before going to sleep. They look forward to the next day's activities and have goals on which to work. They see problems as opportunities and challenges. They have a purpose for getting up in the morning.

Tonight, choose quality sleep.

DON'T . . .

1. Watch violence on television
2. Listen to, or watch, the late evening news
3. Drink coffee or other beverages with caffeine in them

Do . . .

1. Reflect on the successes you've had that day
2. Look forward to something positive, exciting, or interesting the next day
3. Have set goals on which to work
4. Think about all the people who supported you emotionally and professionally that day
5. Visualize yourself waking up alert, cheerful, refreshed, and in a positive state of mind!

It's Your Choice—Quantity . . . or Quality?

MAKING WAVES

As you go through various sleep stages, you experience corresponding frequencies of brainwave activity. Zero to four cycles (brainwave frequencies) per second is the deepest level of unconsciousness and is called the delta level. Four to seven cycles per second are in the theta level. Seven to fourteen cycles per second compose the alpha level. And fourteen cycles or more per second make up the beta level, which is our conscious, awake state.

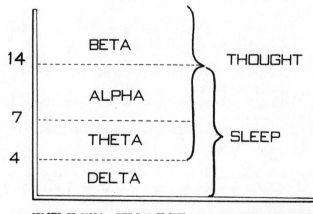

BRAIN WAVE PATTERNS

Every night as you're falling asleep you drift down through a very peaceful mental state of alpha. At this level, your brainwave frequencies become slower, your temperature may drop, and you feel drowsy, though still awake. You're also in the alpha level when you're dreaming. During this light sleep state, you experience rapid eye movements (REM). During REM sleep, your eyes move rapidly underneath your eyelids as though you're watching the action of your dreams. When researchers awaken sleepers during REM sleep, the subjects have easy and often total recall of the dreams they were just having.

After drifting down through the beta and alpha states, you slip into even deeper levels of sleep, theta and delta. Then you might rise up again into alpha for another dream. During a normal night's sleep, you repeat this pattern several times, with each cycle lasting approximately one and one-half hours. When you're wide awake, you're in the beta brainwave state again.

When you have a high-quality nap or meditation, you settle into the alpha level for a while, then awaken feeling refreshed and clear-thinking. If you sleep too long, however, you may drift all the way down into delta. At the delta level, your brainwave frequencies are the slowest. If your alarm clock should sound while you're in this state, your transition into beta is too sudden; you may awaken feeling sluggish and find it hard to get going.

When you learn to control your alpha brainwave patterns, you can enjoy enormous benefits and experience many of the same rewards of having had a long, restful, quality sleep. At the alpha level, you will notice, too, that you have a greater tolerance for stress. You feel less pressured and more relaxed. When you return to work after an alpha break, you experience increased concentration, a longer attention span, more clarity in your thinking, and you can solve problems in less time. In general, you simply feel better about your day.

THE SPEED-SLEEPING TECHNIQUE—HOW TO GET THE EQUIVALENT OF TWO HOURS SLEEP IN TEN MINUTES

You may wish to put the following instructions on a tape to play to yourself whenever you need a break. Or, you may want to read it through and memorize the technique to use whenever you desire.

Close your eyes. Take a deep breath through your nose and exhale through your mouth. Tense your leg muscles as tightly as you can and hold that tension . . . hold it . . . hold it . . . and release it.

Tighten the muscles in your lower back and stomach . . . tighten . . . tighten . . . tighten . . . and release them.

Tighten the muscles in your chest and shoulders . . . tighten . . . tighten . . . tighten . . . and release them.

Tighten your hands into fists. Concentrate on that tension and hold it . . . hold it . . . hold it . . . and release it.

Tense the muscles in your neck, jaw, mouth, scalp, and face. Feel the tension . . . tension . . . tension . . . and release it. Relax the muscles about your eyes, scalp, and face.

Take an inventory of your body. Are there any muscle groups you've forgotten? Tense them. Release them. And relax them.

Now, with your eyes closed, create within your mind an imaginary screen. Then see on that screen the number "3" as you inhale and the word "relax" as you exhale. With every breath you take, you relax more and more.

Next, visualize the number "2" as you inhale and the word "relax" as you exhale.

And finally, see the number "1" as you inhale and the word "relax" as you exhale.

After you are deeply relaxed, create for yourself an escalator going down ten levels, with each descending level causing you to feel a deeper state of relaxation. If you'd rather go up instead of down, simply visualize yourself riding up and farther away.

From now on, whenever you want to relax, get on your mental escalator. You can make your journey even more enjoyable by adding soft music in your mind and pleasing colors.

As you move to each new level, you are relaxing more and more, relaxing more than ever before.

When you arrive at the end of your escalator, you discover your ideal sleeping place where you can enjoy the equivalent of two hours' sleep in ten minutes. Your sleeping place may be a warm, grassy meadow, or a hammock between two trees. It might be a comfortable place on a sunny beach, or in a big bed, or on a cloud. Whatever feels restful to you will be your special place whenever you want to rest. Make it as perfect and as comfortable as you can.

Now create a clock that will awaken you in a very pleasant way. It could be a clock that plays beautiful music or it might be a little cuckoo clock. Set your clock to wake you up in two hours.

Relax and enjoy this beautiful sleeping place—this perfect place where you can receive so much benefit. How beautiful it is to relax!

If your mind wanders, simply focus on your breathing, visualize the number "1" as you inhale, and the word "relax" as you exhale.

Visualize your clock and see that the hands have moved about an hour. You have a whole hour left in this wonderful, pleasant state.

Think the number "1" as you inhale, and the word "relax" as you exhale. Keeping your eyes closed, visualize yourself waking up alert, clear-minded, and super-intelligent, with your natural genius shining through.

Visualize the face of your clock. Fifteen minutes to go . . . ten minutes . . . five minutes more . . . see the hands moving . . . one minute to go.

Begin to count to five and as you count, become more awake and alert. When you reach three, open your eyes. When you reach five, you are fully awake and alert.

1. Becoming more awake and alert.
2. More and more conscious.
3. Open your eyes and blink rapidly several times. Take a deep breath.
4. Wide awake now!
5. Totally alert and refreshed!

Welcome back to a great day!

Why do you think they call it an *alarm* clock in the first place? If you're in the deepest levels of sleep when the alarm goes off, it can jar you rudely to consciousness, leaving you groggy and disoriented. It's better for you to awaken gradually and fully.

1. As you drift off into sleep, state firmly, "Tomorrow I wake up at_____A.M." (State the time you wish to awaken.)
2. Visualize the hands of the clock at the time you wish to awaken.
3. Mentally see yourself waking up refreshed, alert, and ready to go!

Your Action Plan

A. Decide what time you'd like to awaken tomorrow. Set your mental alarm clock this evening.
B. Use your speed-sleeping technique on a daily basis to reduce stress, relax, and refresh your mind and body.
C. Now close this book. Let your body be in a comfortable position. Begin practicing your speed-sleeping technique.

QUOTES TO CONSIDER

"Rest is the sauce of labor."

—Plutarch

"Oh sleep! It is a gentle thing,
Beloved from pole to pole!"

—Samuel Taylor Coleridge

"Sleep is pain's easiest salve . . . ."

—John Donne

"That we are not much sicker and much madder than we are is due exclusively to that most blessed and blessing of all natural graces, sleep."

—Aldous Huxley

12

HOW TO HAVE HIGH-PAYOFF MEETINGS

OBJECTIVES

When you finish this chapter, you will be able to:

- Make meetings wise investments
- Compute the hidden cost of your meetings
- Find effective alternatives to holding meetings
- Set time limits on meetings
- Start meetings on time
- End meetings on time
- Keep meetings dynamic

How many hours do you spend in meetings at work in a typical year? Be sure to count all the informal, one-to-one meetings as well as staff meetings and required company gatherings. How much of that time is personally productive and well spent? Most business people estimate that at least *half* of the time they spend in meetings is wasted time.

Meetings can be very expensive time-wise. To demonstrate this, multiply the wasted minutes of a meeting (starting late, unnecessary socializing, going off on tangents) by the number of people in attendance.

Minutes Wasted	People Present	Total Time Wasted
10 min.	6	60 min. or 1 hour
10 min.	12	120 min. or 2 hours
15 min.	16	240 min. or 4 hours

Meetings are also expensive dollar-wise. To compute the cost of your meetings, add the hourly wage of each attendee. Then multiply this dollar figure times how long the meeting takes.

Hourly Wages	Length of Meeting	Cost of Meeting
Person:		
#1 = $15	1 hour	$125.00
#2 = $35	2 hours	$250.00
#3 = $50 }$125	2½ hours	$312.50
#4 = $25		

DON'T HOLD A $250 MEETING FOR A $25 DECISION. The time invested should equal the dollar yield of the meeting.

QUESTIONS TO ASK BEFORE CALLING A MEETING

	YES	NO
1. Is the time invested in this meeting going to equal the dollar yield of the meeting?	___	___
2. Are my objectives clear for having the meeting?		
a. Do I need advice from all the people who will attend?	___	___
b. Do I need to obtain multiple points of view?	___	___
c. Do I need group involvement to make a decision or to solve a problem?	___	___
d. Do I need a group vote to approve new policies?	___	___
e. Do I need to instruct, train, or educate the group in new methods?	___	___
3. Are there cheaper, faster, or more convenient ways to accomplish the same results?		
a. Could I send staff memos instead?	___	___
b. Could I print-out routine items and let people read them in their spare time?	___	___

c. Could representatives from each department be sent to the   ____   ____
meeting rather than have everyone attend?

d. Could I distribute the information and ask people to respond in   ____   ____
writing and return their comments to me by a certain date?

e. Could I use a telephone conference call instead?   ____   ____

f. Could I speak to people individually instead of in a group?   ____   ____

g. Could the department have fewer meetings? For example,   ____   ____
could weekly meetings be condensed into monthly meetings?

HAVE THE MEETING?   ____   ____

If you decide *not* to have the meeting, list your alternatives below.

_____

_____

_____

If you decide to have the meeting, continue to the next checklist.

	YES	NO
1. Do I have a clear objective for holding the meeting? *Objective:*_____	____	____
2. Have I asked just the key people to attend: those people who will contribute directly to fulfilling the objective?	____	____
3. Do I have an agenda?	____	____
4. Have I written the essential points on the agenda?		
a. The meeting's objectives?	____	____
b. The items to be discussed?	____	____
c. The decisions to be made?	____	____
d. The problems to be solved?	____	____
e. Time limits for discussing each item?	____	____

5. Do I have enough lead time to distribute the agenda at least
twenty-four hours in advance so people can be prepared to contribute?

START ON TIME

When meetings start late, those people who have arrived on time are penalized and they may resent the delay. If punctuality is not reinforced, unspoken, hidden agreements might arise among participants that it's okay to be ten or fifteen minutes late. However, meetings that begin on time in a professional, businesslike manner are likely to continue in that vein. Set the tone of a quality meeting by always starting on time.

To encourage punctuality, consider some of the incentives below.

1. Don't review material in the meeting for latecomers. This only caters to them by giving them attention. It also wastes the time of the people who already heard the information once.
2. Charge 75¢ for each minute a person is late. Put the money into a company fund.
3. Lock the door after the meeting has started.
4. Put the refreshments away once the meeting begins.
5. Have the last person in the door be responsible for typing up and distributing the minutes.

You also might consider starting meetings at odd times such as 9:57 instead of 10 o'clock sharp, since people may attach greater significance to an unusual time.

WHEN YOU'RE IN CHARGE

As the chairperson, you have a great deal of influence over the success of meetings. Use it!

Before the meeting
1. Is the meeting room comfortable?
   a. Can the movie screen, flip charts, and other visuals clearly be seen from all the seats in the room?
   b. Is the lighting good?
   c. Does the sound system work?
   d. If smoking is allowed, is there a nonsmoking section as well?
   e. If the meeting is being held in a hotel or a restaurant, do you have the names and phone numbers of the people who are responsible for room setup should you need anything during the meeting?
2. Are the chairs arranged to enhance the purpose of the meeting?
3. Did you distribute the agenda well in advance so attendees can be prepared to contribute?

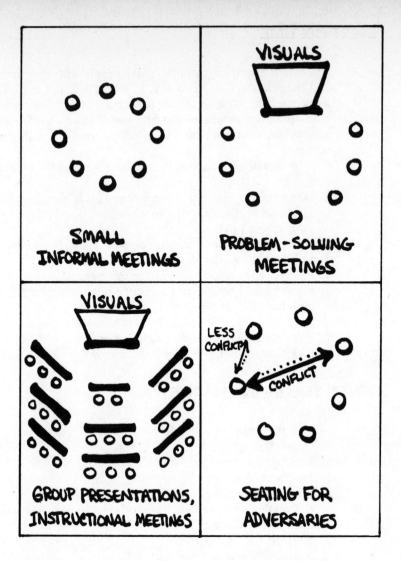

During the meeting

1. Get people involved.
2. Use visual aids.
3. Make use of outside speakers and consultants if appropriate. This lends variety as well as additional expertise to meetings.
4. Set time limits on agenda items. Adhere strictly to the time allotted for discussing each item. If new topics arise, make a note to discuss them in future meetings. Stay on target. Discourage socializing.
5. Respect the ideas of participants. They'll be more likely to contribute if you welcome their suggestions.
6. Don't have calls put through to the meeting room unless they are urgent.
7. Keep meetings positive. End on an "up note" if possible to help keep morale high.

WHEN YOU'RE A PARTICIPANT

Be sure that as a participant, you're not part of the problem of nonproductive meetings. Just as the chairperson is responsible to conduct a successful meeting, you too are responsible for adding to the quality of that meeting.

1. Ask that agendas be distributed at least a day in advance. Come prepared to contribute your ideas and your expertise.
2. Be on time.
3. Speak when spoken to. Don't whisper to others during the presentation. Save socializing until later.
4. Keep your comments brief and to the point.
5. If the meeting's boring, don't sit and resent. That's paying the toll twice. If people are on tangents, ask that the item be brought to a vote. Ask leading questions to return the meeting to its target. Or, entertain yourself by adding to your knowledge of people. Study the group dynamics and the body language of those in attendance.
6. Have your secretary screen calls and hold your messages until the meeting adjourns.

HOW TO SHORTEN MEETINGS

Have you ever noticed how quickly you can wrap things up when the meeting's almost over and you still have four items to cover? Meetings often contract (or expand) to fill the time allotted for them. Shorten meetings, but cover the same amount of material. For example, if a meeting usually goes from 10 A.M. until 12:30 P.M., the next time, hold it from 10:30 A.M. until 12:30 P.M.

Consider having *stand-up* meetings. Remove the chairs from the room. It's more difficult for people to be passive when they're standing up. They'll be more likely to get involved and to stay on target.

Hold meetings before lunch or before quitting time. This is an incentive for people to stay on target and not to run overtime.

END ON TIME

If you start meetings on time, eliminate unnecessary socializing, and faithfully observe the time limit assigned for discussing agenda items, chances are that your meetings will run smoothly and end on time. If certain personnel need to know additional information, allow the others to leave and return to work.

The Challenge	Solutions
Latecomers	Don't confront them publicly. If being late is a habitual problem with them, meet them privately and find out what's going on.
	If they have reports to deliver to the group, schedule their presentations early in the agenda.
	Have your secretary call them in advance to remind them of upcoming meetings.
Low-energy groups	Get people involved. Use the brainstorming technique when appropriate.
	Ask for their feedback: Do they need further clarification on certain points? Could your presentation move faster? Are they ready for a break?
	Be positive, open to their ideas, receptive, and nonjudgmental. Create a safe atmosphere in which they can contribute their ideas.
	Have stretch breaks as well as regular breaks.
	Make sure they understand the objectives for the meeting. What are you all planning to accomplish? How will the results benefit them?
	Hold stand-up meetings. Remove the chairs from the room beforehand. People will get to the point faster as their feet get tired.
	Polish your own presentation and speaking skills. Study a tape of your voice and find ways to make it more interesting. If possible, study yourself on a videotape. Attend other speakers' programs and observe the effectiveness of their styles.
When two or three participants insist on arguing with each other	Don't let it continue if it's counterproductive. Suggest that they continue their discussion on their own time after the meeting.
When the whole group is arguing	Summarize the different points of view. Bring the item to a vote or table it for another meeting to allow participants to mull over the ideas.
Distractions	Arrange the room so people enter from the back. In restaurants, have the coffee service held until after the business portion of the meeting. Get the group to agree to have all calls held unless it's an emergency.

The Challenge	Solutions
Long-winded talkers	When these people stop to catch their breath, break in, summarize briefly, and invite the opinions of others.
	Set time limits on agenda items and on the talking.
Negative people	Don't argue with them or defend yourself. Validate their feelings: "I can see that you're frustrated and impatient. . . . You don't think this idea will work. . . ." Then ask for other points of view from the group. Ask the negative person for his or her positive suggestions.
	Stress the importance of suspending judgment until all the ideas are considered and/or the strategies have been demonstrated.
When the meeting goes off on a tangent	Refer the group back to the agenda.
	Ask leading questions referring to the meeting's objectives.
	Suggest that the new items be discussed at the end of the meeting if there's time or that the ideas be added to the next agenda.
When one or two people keep coming and going during the meeting	If it's a group that meets regularly, meet privately with the offenders and tell it like it is: "I really get distracted when you keep leaving the room. I think it draws from the energy and focus of the group, too. Maybe you and I could brainstorm ways to reduce these interruptions."
	Have a group vote on holding all calls and messages unless there's an emergency.
	If it's a one-time meeting, speak to the person during the break and attempt to eliminate further interruptions for the duration of the meeting.
The loner in the back of the room	Encourage the person who is sitting alone to move forward into the group energy.
	Socialize with this person during the break. She or he might have good ideas to contribute but may be shy about speaking up in a group.

HOW TO
INSTANTLY APPOINT A CHAIRPERSON

At the count of three, everyone in the group points to someone else in the group. The person with the most points has been *a-pointed*.

TIPS ON
BRAINSTORMING

When you want to generate a lot of ideas quickly to solve problems, use the brainstorming techniques:

1. Work in a small group of six to ten people.
2. Sit in a semicircle or a U-shape with a flip chart in front of the group.
3. Appoint a person to record the ideas on the flip chart.
4. As the ideas are recorded, and the flip chart sheets are filled, they are torn off and taped across the front of the room so the ideas remain visible.
5. No one evaluates any of the ideas at this time. In a nonjudgmental atmosphere, people feel free to contribute whatever comes into their minds in the way of solutions. In turn, these ideas give rise to more ideas.
6. When the given time is up, the group discusses the ideas and chooses the top three or four to consider further.
7. After the group has had time to think about the ideas, a second meeting is called for more discussion and a vote.

Your Action Plan

A. Brainstorm ways to improve future meetings.
B. Invent creative strategies for beginning and ending meetings on time.
C. Find alternatives to having meetings.

"The length of a meeting rises with the square of the number of people present."

—Eileen Shanahan

"A committee is a group that keeps the minutes and loses hours."

—Milton Berle

13

WHY ME? DELEGATING

OBJECTIVES

When you finish this chapter, you will be able to:

- Identify the benefits to you for delegating
- Identify your personal barriers to delegating
- Control projects that you delegate by allowing time cushions, evaluating the risk factor, and setting deadlines
- Build employee commitment to a project
- Delegate more work than you thought possible
- Train others to delegate to you more effectively

The role of management is to get things done through others. Delegating is the act of authorizing others to oversee and carry out projects and tasks.

Delegating frees you to be more productive and creative. It establishes you and your subordinates as a team and allows them a measure of professional growth. Delegating forces you to be more organized because you have to outline projects, assign responsibilities to those people most qualified to handle them, set deadlines, and check the progress of subordinates along the way.

Delegating does not absolve you of responsibility. You're still accountable. But with some initial perseverance, you will be able to train subordinates to carry out more and more responsibility, to gain confidence in their abilities, and to free up some of your valuable time.

List all the benefits to you for delegating.

1. _____

2. _____

3. _____

4. _____

5. _____

6. _____

BLOCKS TO DELEGATING

In spite of the many advantages for skillful delegating, many people still resist it. Some people figure that if they want something done right, they have to do it themselves. Some want total control of projects while others fear they may be imposing on subordinates if they ask them to do the work. Some people are afraid that their subordinates will do a better job and maybe take over their positions some day. Still other managers and executives lack confidence in their subordinates, or they feel too busy to train others to take on more responsibility.

Do you find yourself declaring, "I would delegate more if only . . . ." or, "I'd delegate, but . . . ." List your personal barriers to delegating.

1. _____

2. _____

3. _____

4. _____

5. _____

6. _____

If you have no one to whom to delegate, make a list of problems that you have when receiving delegation from others. For example, maybe your boss assigns you trivia and doesn't explain the big picture. Perhaps you don't feel important or you're not motivated to do the work. Maybe your boss dumps everything on you at the last minute and says that everything is top priority.

1. _____

2. _____

3. _____

4. _____

5. _____

6. _____

IF I'M ABSENT, WHO WILL . . .

Failure to delegate sometimes results in employee dependence on you. What if you miss a few days or you're too busy to do everything yourself? Who is there to carry on in your absence?

Make a list of your repetitive duties. First decide if it's necessary that they be done in the first place, then find some area in each that you can give away. There's almost always some part of every project that you can assign to others, even if it's only choosing the kinds of report folders to use.

REPETITIVE JOBS   DELEGATE

_____   _____

_____   _____

_____   _____

_____   _____

Always be on the lookout for *challenging* jobs as well as smaller tasks you can delegate. When you give someone else the opportunity to learn your job, you'll be free to move on to better things. One of the best ways to advance your career is not to look up the ladder, but to look *down* the ladder and help those beneath you. If you keep looking up, you'll create a vacuum that will pull you back down. Allow others their natural brilliance and don't hog the credit. This gives subordinates a sense of their importance to you and to the job. If they're actively involved, they enjoy greater work satisfaction.

When you delegate, be familiar with the workload of others so you aren't overwhelming them with your requests. Prepare them well in advance for bigger jobs so they are ready to help.

Build employee commitment to the job by giving them the big picture of the project and how their services contribute. Be quick to praise, slow to criticize, and, by all means, be interested in the results. It can be discouraging for an employee to spend time with a project and not receive acknowledgment for the effort. Proper appreciation can help assure you of cooperation the next time, too.

CLARIFY YOUR EXPECTATIONS

Clearly outline your expectations before the project is begun and share the objectives with people who are going to be helping you. Divide the project into segments and specify deadlines for each. Communicate what you expect in terms of measureable outcomes. While this may sound like a lot of preparation, it's what you would do if you were handling the total project yourself.

Designate the degree of authority you are delegating. Will your subordinates be doing just research, preparing the first draft or the final draft, making recommendations to you, or working entirely by themselves with the exception of your final approval?

PROJECT CONTROL

Allow time cushions so if something unexpected goes wrong you'll have time to correct it. Set up project checkpoints along the way. This allows subordinates the freedom to fail and all is not lost. There will be plenty of time to correct errors, and employees can learn from the experience.

Evaluate the risk factor of delegating by asking yourself, "What's the worst that can go wrong?" If the worst is very bad, monitor the project closely or don't delegate at all.

DELAY CRITICISM

After others have completed a project for you, praise them for all the good work. If they did something you didn't like, delay your criticism until the beginning of the next project. Someone may have spent all night preparing a report and doesn't need to be told that the printing job is bad. Before the next project, recommend a different printer.

AVOID UPWARD DELEGATION

Upward delegation occurs when your subordinates have you doing their work for them. For example, someone might say to you, "As long as you are here now, would you return Ms. Smith's call since you are more familiar with her account than I am?" or, "Since you're going to copy that report on the way home, could you take these items with you and duplicate them, too?"

In many situations, upward delegation results from employee overdependence on you, a need you've probably fostered by not delegating in the first place. In other cases, employees lack confidence in themselves. I once had an assistant who always had a million questions for me. I knew that, given a little time, she could figure out the answers herself. At first, it seemed that I was saving time because I could quickly tell her the answers. I finally realized that she was continuously interrupting me and that in the long run I was wasting a great deal of time.

Eventually, I told this assistant to come to me with three answers to each of her questions. I instructed her to rate the solutions according to the ones she thought were best. Then we could discuss them. She always came up with the right answers, thereby instilling confidence in herself and my trust in her abilities.

WHEN YOU'RE THE DELEGATE

If you're not getting delegated to as you'd like, you may be partially at fault. Do you passively accept poor delegation, incomplete instructions, too many projects at a time, unclear deadlines? There are a number of things you can do to make it easier on yourself when you receive delegation.

1. Find out how much authority you have on assignments. Once you clarify the degree of authority you have, you can carry out the project without constant approval from your boss.

2. Whenever possible, offer your boss solutions to problems that have arisen while you are doing the assigned work. This allows you to exercise your own creativity and initiative. It may strengthen your working relationship with your boss and possibly give you an edge when people are being considered for promotions.

3. Repeat directions in your own words so you and your boss are certain you've understood the assignment correctly.

4. Ask for specific deadlines for each major part of the project.

5. If your boss procrastinates or is reluctant to give you authority, write up your proposed action plan and submit it to your boss with an "Unless I hear otherwise" memo: "Dear Boss, unless I hear otherwise from you by such and such a date, I will go ahead and . . ."

6. Make your boss aware of how disruptive last-minute projects can be when you're already working flat out. If your boss dumps everything on you at the last minute, show her or him your to-do list. Ask where the additional items can fit in.

7. If your boss overwhelms you with work, have her or him prioritize what needs to be done. See if you can reschedule projects and deadlines in order to accommodate the workload.

8. Ask your boss how well the job has to be done. Is it necessary for you to put a dollar's worth of effort into a penny project?

If you're feeling pressured and have no one to whom to delegate during a project, you can still enlist the support of some very knowledgable people. Librarians can offer valuable assistance with research. You also can request the services of outside consultants for special projects, or temporary help when things are especially hectic.

DO YOU CHARGE AHEAD INSTEAD OF DELEGATING?

Your Action Plan

For the next three weeks, when you plan your to-do list, write why me? after each item and figure out how you can delegate it.

"To be good is noble, but to teach others how to be good is nobler
. . . and much less trouble."

—Mark Twain

14

DECISIONS, DECISIONS, DECISIONS!

When you finish this chapter, you will be able to:

- Evaluate how decisive you are
- Make quality decisions
- Improve your decisiveness
- Apply several powerful strategies to help you make your next decision
- Tap into your natural decision-making abilities

How decisive are you? Write down a number from 1 to 10, number 1 being the least decisive and number 10 the most decisive: _____. If you're like some people, you may have felt the urge to turn to others for their opinions: "How decisive do you think I am? Do you think I'm a 5 or a 6, or maybe a 7? Could I be a 7?" If you wanted to ask someone else, subtract 3 points from your score on the following questionnaire.

How Decisive Are You?

	OFTEN (1)	SOMETIMES (2)	RARELY (3)	NEVER (4)
1. Do you have second thoughts after making decisions?	___	___	___	___
2. Do the opinions of others unduly influence your decisions?	___	___	___	___
3. Do you procrastinate on making decisions?	___	___	___	___
4. Do you agonize over making difficult decisions?	___	___	___	___
5. Do you bog down considering so many details that it's hard for you to decide?	___	___	___	___
6. Do you put a dollar's worth of energy into making a one-cent decision?	___	___	___	___
7. Have you missed opportunities because you waited too long to decide?	___	___	___	___
8. Do you let others decide for you on choices that are really yours to make?	___	___	___	___
9. Did you hesitate as you answered these questions?	___	___	___	___

Your Score

Give yourself 1 point for each *often* you checked, 2 points for each *sometimes,* 3 points for each *rarely,* and 4 points for each *never.* Add up your points and find your score on the scale below.

32–36: Most likely, your life is working the way you'd like it to. You have long-term goals, you take responsibility for your choices in life, and you are quite decisive.

20–31: Making decisions may be uncomfortable for you. Sometimes you're hot, sometimes you're cold when it comes to making decisions. To be more consistently decisive, look for tips in this chapter.

Below 19: You need to be more decisive. Chances are, you're sitting on a major decision right now. You may be hoping that it will go away or that someone else will make the decision for you. To gain more self-confidence in your natural decision-making ability, apply the strategies in this chapter.

Every day you make hundreds of decisions. The quality of your life equals the sum total of those decisions: whether or not to exercise, what to have for breakfast, when to go to work, whether or not to ask for a raise or to change jobs, etc.

The decisions you make are the results of previous decisions you've made and past experiences you've had. When you're confronted with a decision, your inner computer scans your memory banks for similar situations and bases your decision on what you've already learned in the past. For example, if your gas gauge is on empty, you remember that the last time that happened you ended up at the side of the road trying to hitch a ride. This time when your gauge is nearly on empty, you decide quickly to drive to the nearest gas station. Thanks to your ability to build upon memories, decision-making is easier and faster.

The times when you have trouble deciding are when you scan your past experiences and discover conflicting information, such as when you made the wrong choices, or when you worry about what others will think of your decisions. In these cases, it's necessary to switch into a different mode of creative decision-making.

Examine your belief systems. A belief system is something we accept as being true without questioning it. Personal belief systems start early in life because our intellects are not developed enough to analyze and screen out many of the things that are done and said to us. For example, a child who has done something incorrectly and who has been criticized for it may feel that as a *person* he or she is no good. Children cannot always rationalize that it was just their *behavior* that was incorrect. When they grow up, they may base their decisions on the irrational belief that they are failures; they may resist accepting more responsibilities at work or they may turn down better job opportunities.

Another fairly common belief is: no pain, no gain. People who subscribe to this belief may set themselves up to always be struggling. When things go right, they may feel that it's too good to be true. Consequently, they may sabotage their success in order to get back into the struggle mode that more closely conforms to their belief system.

Examine your belief systems regarding prosperity, work, friends, and your self-image. Are you basing today's decisions on old beliefs that may be invalid?

Set goals. If you know where you are and where you're going, you'll have no problem deciding which turns to make to get there. However, if you're like Alice in Wonderland and have no goals, you could waste a lot of time:

"Would you tell me, please, which way I ought to go from here?"
"That depends a good deal on where you want to get to," said the Cat.
"I don't care much where—" said Alice.
"Then it doesn't matter which way you go," said the Cat.
"—so long as I get *somewhere,*" Alice added as an explanation.
"Oh, you're sure to do that," said the Cat, "if you only walk long enough."

In your own life, you might struggle with a particular decision: should I quit my job, ask for a raise, go here, go there, do business with certain people? Once you've clarified your long-range goals and objectives in life, these decisions become easier. For example, if it's your career goal to become a computer programmer, you'd make decisions that would move you closer to that goal: which courses to take, what kind of equipment to buy, which materials to read, what people to meet. Having goals gives your life meaning. With a goal in mind, you have a sense of purpose. Your daily activities count for something.

Clarify your values. What do you value in life? Make decisions appropriate to those values. For example, if you value friendship, turn off the television and go some place where you'll meet people.

Do you value education, career enhancement, self-improvement, physical fitness, wealth? What decisions are you making regarding those things? Align the way you live and work with what you value.

HOW TO IMPROVE YOUR DECISIVENESS

Write down a decision you've been wanting to make:

_____

Follow each of the steps below, and by the end of this section you may be pleasantly surprised to discover that you have made your decision.

Clearly define your goal. Make your goal specific and measurable. For example, instead of saying that you want to exercise more, write down that you want to jog at least one mile three days a week.

_____

Research. When making a decision, use both primary and supplementary sources. Primary sources provide you with valuable, first-hand information. For example, if you're trying to decide whether or not to begin a jogging program, consult a doctor or two regarding the benefits and precautions of jogging, and talk to several people who already jog. Then read supplementary sources for a good overall picture: exercise books, health journals, and magazines for runners.

If you're trying to decide which personal computer to buy, talk with sales representatives from three or four computer companies. Ask these salespeople to tell you what they know about their competitors' models and you're sure to gain some interesting insights. You also might want to talk with people who are already using certain computers that interest you. When you've researched a number of primary sources, then supplement what you've learned by reading several computer journals.

List some primary sources you can consult for the decision you want to make.

_____

_____

_____

_____

_____

_____

List some supplementary sources that would be helpful for you to read.

_____

_____

_____

_____

_____

As you conduct your research, recognize the point of diminishing returns. If you attempt to consult all the experts in the field and read all the available material, the return on your invested time will begin to diminish. Sooner or later, you simply have to make your decision.

Evaluate the risk. Sometimes people are afraid of making decisions because they fear the consequences. If this is the case, ask yourself, "What's the worst that can happen if I decide a certain way?" If the worst is very bad, don't dwell on it; put some more research time into the decision and find a few more alternatives. Often the worst thing that can happen is that you'll learn from the experience—and that's not a serious consequence! Mistakes can be stepping stones to wisdom.

Examine what's the worst that can happen if you make the "wrong" decision.

_____

_____

_____

_____

At one time, I was deliberating on whether or not to relocate my business from California to Texas. While moving involved a great deal of work on my part, I realized that the rewards of moving were worth the risks. As it turned out, relocating was a wise decision. Had it been the "wrong" decision, I could have moved somewhere else more suitable. True, it would have taken more work to move again, but I found some comfort in knowing that my decision was reversible.

Louise H., a writer who was working as an administrative assistant, was offered an opportunity to work as a training consultant for a new firm. The second job promised a considerable raise for working fewer hours. However, since the company was new, its future was uncertain. Louise was confronted with a major decision: whether to opt for job security, or to take a chance on a new job that might fall through after a few months. She remembered that her goal in life was to have enough time and money to work as a writer. She hoped eventually to support herself as a writer. The job as a consultant would allow her the time and money to write.

Then Louise considered the worst that could happen: The job might fall through and leave her unemployed. She was confident, however, that she could find another job as an administrative assistant. She also concluded that if one company wanted her as a consultant, there might be others out there as well who would hire her. She chose to take the second job and is doing very well.

Surprisingly, making mistakes can lead to success. Some of the most successful people make more mistakes than people who plod along and play it safe. An example of this can be seen when we consider Babe Ruth. At one time, he held the record for making the most home runs. *At the same time,* he was also the strike-out king! His willingness to strike out more often than anyone else enabled him to hit more home runs and surpass all previous records.

Avoid paralysis of analysis. If you go over and over things in your mind when you try to make a decision, if you're torn this way and that by conflicting thoughts, you may be suffering from paralysis of analysis. Stop mulling over your problems. Sort out your thinking by using an excellent decision-making technique described by Ben Franklin over two hundred years ago: To avoid circular thinking, write down all your reasons *for* a particular decision and all your reasons *against* it; compare the pros and cons and make your decision.

To update Ben Franklin's strategy, assign a weight to each pro and con, with the number 10 being the most important and number 1 the least important. Then make a list of alternative ways to solve the challenge. The example below is the worksheet of an accounting executive who was trying to decide whether or not to buy a new car. Study what he did, then follow the same procedure on the following page for your decision.

Goal: To get to work every day on time.
Decision: Whether or not to buy a new car.

for	weight	against	weight
A new car would be more reliable than the old one	8	My old car still runs fairly well	8
I would feel better with a new car	7	New models will be out in 2 months; if I wait, I'll get a better deal	8
A new car would improve my image	5	I have a poor credit rating	10
Score:	20	Score:	36

Alternatives to buying a new car:

1. Put $ into repairing old car. _____

2. Car pool to save money. _____

3. To improve image, rent a luxury car when entertaining clients. ___

Goal: _____

Decision: _____

for	weight	against	weight
1. _____			
_____			
2. _____			
_____			
3. _____			
_____			
4. _____			
_____			

_____

_____

_____

_____

Ask the world's greatest authority. Tune into your own genius and your natural decision-making ability. Regarding the decision you want to make, ask yourself, "What would the world's greatest authority advise me in this situation?" This approach helps to detach you from a limited viewpoint and tap into that inner brilliance that knows what's best for you.

What would the world's greatest authority advise *you* about your decision?

_____

_____

_____

_____

Do something. Army officers are advised that when they are in danger, any action, no matter how poorly conceived or poorly executed, is preferable to no action at all. In other words, *do something!*

It might be that you decide *not* to decide at the present. If this is the case, give yourself a time limit for when you *will* make a choice. This strategy worked well for a husband and wife who were considering a separation. They felt that both of them were too emotional at the time to think clearly, so they postponed their decision for three months. Since the pressure was off for a while, they found it easier to communicate and began to enjoy each other more. When it came time to decide on the separation, they chose to stay together.

Whatever you do, decide something. If you're in a dark room and you do nothing, you'll remain in the dark. But if you feel for the wall and start to move along it, eventually you'll find a doorway, a window, or a light switch.

Your Action Plan

Use the Ben Franklin decision-making strategy on the next decision you want to make.

___QUOTE TO CONSIDER___

"You don't have a problem—you just have a decision to make."
—Robert Schuller

15

THE FLAWS
OF
PERFECTIONSM
THE FLAWS
OF
PERFECTONISM
THE FLAWS
OF
PERFECTIONISM

When you finish this chapter, you will be able to:

- Spot your perfectionistic tendencies
- Break the pattern of perfectionism
- Overcome perfectionism in reading, writing, and delegating
- Gain personal insights into perfectionism

Do you worry about what others think of you?

Do you postpone making important calls for fear of being rejected?

Do you do things over and over to get them *just right?*

Does it take you forever to get things done—and even then, do you find they're not quite the way you wanted them?

Do you feel good about yourself when you do well and depressed when you don't?

Do you measure your self-worth in terms of your outstanding achievements?

If you answered "Yes" to any of the above, you may be a victim of self-inflicted perfectionism.

It's good to be interested in quality, but you must also be fair with yourself. Compulsive striving for unrealistic goals can impair your creativity, cause tension between you and others, and waste valuable time. Is it worth the price? Or is it time to break these self-defeating patterns?

THE ROOTS OF PERFECTIONISM

Perfectionism has its beginnings early in life when children are compared to others. To please teachers and parents, many children strive for academic and athletic excellence. Advertisements show how perfect life can be when our cars are faster, our breaths are fresher, and our whites are whiter. Perfectionists have learned to measure their self-worth in terms of their achievements and, consequently, dread being *average*. Meanwhile, their nonperfectionistic colleagues are making more money, closing important deals, and getting things done much faster.

HOW TO BREAK THE PATTERN

There's a point in all endeavors when the return on your invested time begins to diminish. For example, when your speech is written, don't waste an hour in the library looking for a quote that might enhance it but isn't necessary. By the same token, don't run all over town looking for a particular report folder when second-best will do. Don't have letters retyped to be picture-perfect; the recipients will just file them or throw them away. Begin to recognize that *below average to a perfectionist is often perfectly acceptable to others*.

In many situations, 20 percent of what you do yields 80 percent of your results. Concentrate on those high-payoff items. Of the remaining low-payoff items, ask yourself, *"What is the least work I can do on these and still have them be acceptable?"* Then determine which activities you can delegate, which require your limited thought, and which demand your careful attention. Act accordingly.

Let your purpose for doing a job determine how much time you spend doing it. For example, if you're going to show a report to colleagues to get their suggestions, don't slave over endless revisions. Chances are, you'll get so much feedback that, by the time you finish incorporating the comments of your co-workers, the report will be unrecognizable anyway. If you'll be giving an oral report, forget about correcting the typos altogether.

When writing for publication, get all your ideas down first. Ignore your meddlesome internal critic (which may actually be the voices of your parents and past teachers), and plunge ahead without censoring yourself. Forget grammar, spelling, and other mechanics of writing until you are satisfied that you've recorded every feeling, thought, and necessary piece of information; then go back, organize, and polish.

When reading, allow your purpose for reading to determine how fast you will read. Read contracts more slowly since they may contain tricky phrases. Read business updates and routine memos quickly.

PERFECTIONISM AND DELEGATING

Do you believe the old adage, "If you want something done right, do it yourself?" If you do, you could be denying others the opportunity to grow, as well as wasting time trying to do everything yourself. Break a project down into its components and decide which parts you can delegate. *Don't ask if others can do the job as well as you, but if they can do the job well enough.* Set up checkpoints to review what's been done and make necessary corrections.

GAIN PERSPECTIVE

Begin to look for shades of correctness in your work. Realize, for example, that a business letter is not all right or all wrong if it isn't typed on letterhead stationery or if it has a corrected typo or two in it. It might be okay for your purposes.

Whenever you feel overwhelmed, get the big picture by asking yourself, "How is this particular day or project going to fit in with the rest of my life? *What will it matter in 150 years?"*

LEARN FROM YOUR MISTAKES

Many people have been raised with the attitude that if something is worth doing, it's worth doing right. Perfectionists further reason that if they can't do something well, they shouldn't do it at all. An example of this faulty thinking can be seen in the salesperson who prefers to stay in the office and work on trivia rather than make calls that might lead to rejection. This person would be better off making calls poorly than doing the wrong thing (trivia) well. *Achievers know that out of doing something poorly can come the experience to do it well later on.*

When you evaluate and learn from your mistakes, you are free to grow. Thomas Edison tried more than one thousand filaments for the light bulb before he found one that worked. When asked about his failures, he stated that he had not failed—he had succeeded in discovering over one thousand filaments that didn't work. With his persistence, he lit the world.

Your Action Plan

A. Identify those items on which you are overly perfectionistic.
B. List tasks you do that others could handle.
C. Be careful not to overdo things unnecessarily.
D. Call mistakes "stepping stones" and see what you can learn from them.

_____QUOTE TO CONSIDER_____

"Friend, don't be a perfectionist. Perfectionism is a curse and a strain."

—Fritz Perls

16

TRAVEL TIME

OBJECTIVES

When you finish this chapter, you will be able to:

- Travel with less stress and more enjoyment
- Cut back travel time preparation
- Keep your energy and productivity high during long commutes
- Evaluate the effectiveness of your trip afterward

As a traveler who logs more than 200,000 miles a year, I have seen it all—from traffic jams, delayed flights, and congested airports to lost luggage, missed connections, and jet lag. In an effort to cope better with all these frustrations, and to make travel less stressful, I've arrived at several basic strategies on how you can pare down your travel preparations, make the most of commuting time, and get to your hotel (or back home) from the airport in one piece.

BEFORE YOUR TRIP

Decide if the trip is necessary. Can you accomplish the same results by sending a letter, telephoning, or making a conference call? Could you delegate the responsibility of the trip to a trusted representative? If you must go, go first to an experienced travel agent.

Use a good travel agent. Travel agents have many contacts not accessible to individual travelers. They can often get you deals and discounts you might miss if you planned your own itinerary.

Always keep a checklist. Record everything that you need for your trip, from vitamins to business materials. Carry the list with you so you'll remember what to pack for your return trip. Make two copies of your itinerary, listing where you can be reached during the trip. Leave one copy at home with your family, and one at the office.

Have alternative travel plans. If you are a frequent flyer, subscribe to the Official Airline Guide (OAG). This valuable resource lists flights for all airlines plus their stopovers, discounts, and food services. If you find yourself in a traffic jam and in danger of missing your flight, simply consult your OAG for the next flight out and drive directly to that airline. If you don't subscribe to the guide, have your travel agent outline alternative travel plans for you. This takes the panic out of missed flights and missed connections.

Avail yourself of a frequent-flyer program. In order to qualify, you have to accumulate a specified amount of flying time with one particular airline. If you *do* qualify, your membership entitles you to special treatment, travel discounts, and many other benefits. For more information, contact the airline's sales office.

Travel lightly. The more you take on board with you, the less you are likely to lose. If possible, condense everything you need into one carry-on case and a garment bag.

Prepare your luggage for easy handling. To eliminate wasted time packing, unpacking, and repacking for each trip, consider keeping an extra set of personal items packed at all times in a separate case. For traveling, invest in a collapsible luggage cart or a suitcase with wheels. This lightens your load considerably in case you cannot find a skycap or a porter. Remove destination labels from previous trips before you check your baggage, and keep your phone number inside in case the outside label is detached en route. Mark your luggage for easy identification at the baggage-claim area.

Carry important numbers with you. Take along the phone numbers of hotels and people you will be visiting. You also may wish to carry the numbers of local businesses and temporary office services in the area. Jot down your credit card numbers and store them in a safe place, along with the receipts for your traveler's checks. This way, the information is on hand if you should need to replace something.

Research temperatures in cities you will be visiting. Postcards do not always tell the truth about climates. For example, that golden fog pictured over San Francisco is usually anything but warm; whenever visiting this fascinating city, take a sweater or jacket for evening wear, even in July. And be prepared for a lot of rain in Seattle, as well as unpredictable weather in the Northeast. Before you leave, check destination-point temperatures by consulting the newspaper and watching the weather reports on television. Pack accordingly.

Never assume anything. Flights may be grounded at the last minute, accidents may cause traffic jams, and hotels may misplace your reservation. Before going to the airport, listen to traffic reports on the radio. Call the airline to find out if your flight is on time and from what gate it will depart. Always confirm your hotel reservations before setting out.

Set up a portable office. Travelers are blessed with uninterrupted time. Make the most of it by equipping your briefcase with office supplies such as stationery, stamps, envelopes, pens, dictating equipment, pocket dictionary, and a calendar. Stock your briefcase with reading material and other work.

Allow for unexpected delays. Surprises are okay for birthday parties, but you want to minimize them when it comes to traveling. Be generous in figuring out how long it will take you to get somewhere. Allow time to buy tickets, travel to the airport or train station, check in and board, claim your luggage afterward, and travel to the hotel. Don't book connecting flights too closely in case the first one is late. Avoid rush hours whenever possible. Plan your arrival time to coincide with lighter traffic.

Avoid jet lag. Go to sleep half an hour earlier or later each night before your trip until you have adjusted to the differences in time zones. Shift mealtimes gradually. Once on board, set your watch for arrival time in the new time zone to prepare yourself psychologically for the change. Drink a lot of water to offset possible dehydration caused by the low humidity aboard planes.

EN ROUTE

Keep on creating. Don't put your creative thinking on hold just because you are in transit. Take advantage of uninterrupted blocks of time to dictate, write part of a book, answer letters, draft articles, or read. If you are commuting in your car, you might want to listen to educational, inspirational, or motivational tapes.

Carry snacks with you. Keep your energy high and your blood sugar stable by carrying nuts, cheese, fruit, or yogurt with you. In that way, storms, traffic jams, and unexpected delays won't interfere with proper nutrition.

AFTERWARD

Avoid the herding instinct. People are pretty territorial and have a tendency to bunch up at the exits to deplane or detrain. Remain in your seat and use the few extra minutes to collect your thoughts and let the crowd clear out.

Get acquainted with the concierge. When you go to your hotel, ask to meet the concierge or bell captain. He or she will be happy to recommend restaurants, help secure theater tickets, and assist with a variety of other problems, such as locating a particular foreign newspaper.

Minimize stress. After a great deal of traveling, eat a light meal, get some exercise if you can, relax and shower (hang your clothes in the bathroom to steam out wrinkles), and go to sleep early. If you have trouble sleeping, eat foods rich in tryptophan, a natural tranquilizer. You'll find tryptophan in poultry, cheese, peanut butter, eggs, and milk. You can also purchase it in capsule form in health food stores.

Evaluate your trip. When your trip is over, write letters commending particularly helpful and pleasant personnel and departments. You will feel better for having expressed your appreciation, and they will be certain to remember your compliments and give you good service the next time, too. Likewise, discontinue using services, hotels, and airlines that have not given you good service. Make note of special travel challenges you experienced. Resolve to find solutions for the next trip that you take.

1. Become aware of all the time you spend commuting. Multiply your daily travel time by the number of days you go to work. Multiply this by the weeks in the month and you have a considerable amount of time! Vow to use this time wisely. You can accomplish a lot with proper planning.

2. Organize commuting time just as you would organize your day at the office. Plan commuting activities in advance. Put them on your daily to-do list. Choose some long-term activities such as learning a new subject or a foreign language (invest in a good tape deck or a portable, battery-run tape recorder). Listen to the tapes every day as you travel. Set goals for yourself. For example, "By the last week in January, I will have learned _____ (how many) foreign vocabulary words."

3. Rehearse speeches, presentations, and interviews.

4. Dictate business letters, friendly notes, and memos.

5. Practice voice exercises.

6. Listen to motivational, inspirational, and musical tapes.

7. Share rides. The company of others can make commuting more pleasant and interesting.

8. Make commuting time exercise time. For example, ride to work and walk home, or get off the bus several stops sooner and walk.

9. Map the best routes. Explore frontage roads. They'll provide you with a change of scenery and may come in handy if you need a detour during heavy traffic.

10. Implement a flextime schedule at work. Work the same amount of time each day, but come in earlier and leave earlier, or come in later and leave later.

11. When moving to a new area, choose a house close to your job or near major transportation lines.

12. Stay relaxed. Don't weave in and out of traffic trying to get to work ten minutes earlier. The time you save may not be worth the stress and pressure that hurrying creates. Make it your goal to get to work (or home) with your energy and your sanity intact.

Your Action Plan

A. Make a checklist for the next trip you take.
B. Decide upon a travel agent to use regularly.
C. Keep important numbers in your wallet so they'll be handy when you travel.
D. Create an office in your briefcase.
D. Call airlines for information on their frequent-flyer programs.
E. Keep an extra set of personal items packed at all times so you don't have to keep unpacking and repacking for trips.

QUOTES TO CONSIDER

"The use of travelling is to regulate imagination by reality, and instead of thinking how things may be, to see them as they are."
—Samuel Johnson

"He who would travel happily must travel light."
—Antoine de Saint-Exupéry

17

WHAT TO DO WHEN YOUR SENSE OF TIME CLASHES WITH OTHERS'

OBJECTIVES

When you finish this chapter, you will be able to:

- Identify sources of resentment, pressure, and tension that originate from conflicting styles of managing time
- Better relate to and work with people who are either more or less organized than you are
- Stay high (legally) all day

In any office, there are likely to be differences in the workers' peak production times, work styles, and time perspectives. Some people are grumpy, scratchy, and crawly in the morning and bright as sunshine after lunch, while others are at their peaks before 10 A.M., but growl like Neanderthals if asked to take on a task in the afternoon.

Some people approach a six-month deadline by starting early and doing a little of the project each day, while others always seem to have a frantic finish.

Some people plan ahead and have plenty of supplies on hand, while others order supplies only when they run out.

Some people keep their work areas clean and well organized, while others let things get hopelessly scattered.

Some people are always punctual, while others consider themselves still on time if they're only fifteen minutes late.

These differences in time-management attitudes and approaches to work are apt to cause resentment, disharmony, or even outright clashes. Here are some suggestions for dealing with the problem.

DON'T JUDGE OTHERS BY YOUR OWN STANDARDS

It's a natural tendency for a person who considers taking breaks a waste of time to be suspicious of those who do take them. And it's also natural for a person who needs breaks to figure that a colleague who doesn't take them is trying to win points with the boss.

If others are goofing off when you're gearing up, or if they're gearing up when you're goofing off, be aware that people's periods of greatest effectiveness are different. Whenever possible, adjust your demands accordingly.

CLARIFY PRIORITIES

When your boss piles on the work and insists that *everything* is top priority, show him or her your time log to illustrate how busy you really are. Then ask your boss to be more specific about which tasks must be done first, second, and third.

Also, have your boss sit down with you and your co-workers to realign your priorities. Maybe the way you or your co-workers have been doing things is no longer the best way. If there are conflicts in priorities, clarify them.

COMMUNICATE

Express how you feel by using "I" messages. For example, you might say, "When we run out of supplies, I find it very disruptive waiting for more to come in or trying to track some down at the last minute. Let's order supplies in advance."

"I" messages enable you to state your feelings clearly and simply without accusing others. This, in turn, may encourage others to express themselves without feeling threatened. Then everyone will have an opportunity to discuss the problem openly.

SHARE IDEAS

At staff meetings, discuss new strategies for managing time. This way, everyone benefits from innovative ideas without feeling personally corrected.

PREPARE FOR OTHERS' HABITS

If your co-workers seem to have deep-rooted bad habits, you might find it easier to change *your* reactions to them, than trying to make them change. Anticipate what others are going to do, based on their past behavior. Adjust your schedule accordingly. For example, if your boss tends to have continual last-minute emergencies for you to solve, anticipate this and don't overschedule your day. Leave time cushions in your plans.

REMEMBER TO PRAISE OTHERS

Most likely, your co-workers are doing *something* right timewise. Find out what it is, and express your appreciation. For example, say, "Thanks for giving me the work early. The extra time helped me do an especially good job on it." Reinforce *positive* behavior and you might see more of it.

WHEN IN DOUBT, TAKE CHARGE

Become less dependent on the whims of others. Tell them, *"Unless I hear otherwise,* I will go ahead and order supplies early, start meetings on time, and set my own priorities on the items you give me to do." Most likely, they'll be too busy to get back to you, and you'll have their implied consent to go ahead and do things in your own time-effective way.

HOW TO STAY HIGH (LEGALLY) ALL DAY

Some days it may seem as though you're on an energy roller coaster—up and down, up and down. Avoid the slumps. Keep your energy level high by following the guidelines below.

Manage by objectives. Stay on target by knowing where you're going. When you have a sense of direction, you keep focused and have a sense of purpose about the day.

Finish fully. Starting new projects is often more interesting and exciting than following through on old ones. However, having a lot of things started at once scatters your thinking, undermines your progress, and drags your energy level down. What you complete gives you a feeling of accomplishment. Finish fully, or at least work to natural stopping places. If you set something down, make a note on what your next step will be so you can return with a minimum of "warm-up" time.

Speed sleep. Take time to relax with a speed sleep break at least once a day. Going flat out all day is not only hard on the body, but on the mind as well. Be kind to yourself. Rid yourself of accumulated tension. Stop for just a few minutes a day to rest and you'll be further ahead by the end of the day.

Plan a realistic to-do list. Overscheduling your day can overwhelm you and drag your energy level down. Why write twenty items on a to-do list if you only have time to finish eight? See Chapters 3–4 for guidelines on how to plan and organize your day.

Make lulls work for you. Plan to do your trivial work during lulls in energy. This way, you still move ahead and are not making excessive demands on your energy level.

Do the worst first. Do the most awful thing that you have to do *first.* Get it out of the way so you can better focus on other tasks throughout the day.

Eat right. Enjoy a substantial breakfast, a light lunch, and an even lighter dinner. Avoid fried foods, sugar, and excessive amounts of caffeine. Exercise regularly, even if it's just walking.

Have a positive attitude. When you follow the above suggestions, you'll find a positive attitude coming more naturally.

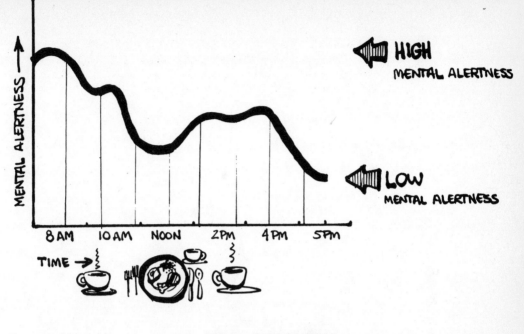

Your Action Plan

A. Analyze the time conflicts between yourself and others. Make a list of what you can do to improve the overall situation.
B. Practice using "I" messages.
C. Do a time log on your day to identify when you are the most productive.
D. Express your appreciation the next time someone uses good time management.
E. At your next staff meeting, share ideas for improving time-management habits.
F. Make a time-metabolism graph showing your highs and lows during the day; compare your graph with the graphs of co-workers.

QUOTES TO CONSIDER

"Adopt the pace of nature; her secret is patience."
—Emerson

"Nothing is more highly to be praised but the value of each day."
—Goethe

18

EFFECTIVE COMMUNICATION

OBJECTIVES

When you finish this chapter, you will be able to:

- Identify the three basic styles of communicators
- Tailor time-saving approaches to each type of communicator
- Establish instant rapport with people
- Communicate without making others feel defensive
- Listen more accurately to others

Communication is the expression and exchange of thoughts and feelings. Failure to communicate clearly can result in lost business, serious misunderstandings, and wasted time.

THREE STYLES OF COMMUNICATING

Problems can arise in communicating because people do not always understand things in the same way. We can save much time communicating with co-workers when we understand the three basic styles of communicating: analytical, emotional, and visual.

Analytical Individuals

These highly articulate people express themselves in complicated sentences and analytical terms. They may use phrases such as, "I think . . ." and, "I understand . . ." Analyzers may be difficult to know. Sometimes, they become workaholics to escape their feelings, which they may have trouble expressing. Analyzers can be very good at communicating concepts and ideas.

List the people you know who are analyzers.

_____

_____

_____

_____

_____

Your time-saving approach for communicating with analyzers: Give these people the facts and get to the point quickly. Analyzers grasp ideas very fast and get bored with long explanations. They respect people who speak accurately, who know the facts, and who are organized in their presentations.

Emotional Individuals

These people wear their hearts on their sleeves and often take on the problems of the world. To recognize this type, look for people who are emotionally involved in other people's problems and who are very loyal to friends, companies, and causes. Emotional individuals often use phrases such as, "This feels right. . . ," "Get in touch with what you're feeling. . . ." and "I sense that this is a good thing. . . ." Because they operate on such a feeling level, these people may have trouble putting their feelings into words.

List the people you know who fit into this category.

_____

_____

_____

_____

_____

Your time-saving approach for communicating with emotional people: Since these individuals have a fascination for details, be sure to give them a lot of details about a project. Be patient when they're expressing their ideas verbally; it may be difficult for them. Be sure to encourage their feedback about projects and be liberal with your positive reinforcement.

Visual Individuals

These communicators are good organizers. Usually very neat, visualizers tend to be perfectionists. They can easily visualize ideas and often use phrases such as, "I get the picture. . . ," "I see what you mean. . . ." and, "Look at this. . . ."

List the people you know who are visualizers.

_____

_____

_____

_____

_____

Your time-saving approach for communicating with visualizers: Give these people the overall picture of a project. Be sure to use a lot of visuals whenever possible. Paint word phrases for visualizers by using descriptive phrases.

HOW TO ESTABLISH INSTANT RAPPORT

To quickly establish mutual trust, identify what type of communicator the person is with whom you're speaking. Then subtly match the person's posture, energy level, and ability to hold or withhold eye contact. This mirroring should not be intrusive or obvious (don't mirror habits such as nervous ticks or stuttering). People who are already in rapport with each other just naturally do this.

Use "I" messages. When people feel defensive, they talk back and argue to justify and rationalize their behavior. To avoid putting others on the defensive, use "I" messages. Instead of saying, "*You* are always late with the monthly report!" say, "I can plan my work schedule more effectively if I know that the monthly report will be on time. Is there anything I can do to help you get it in by the fifteenth of each month?" People will be more receptive to your suggestions if they don't feel that they've been attacked and criticized.

Ask for feedback. Don't assume anything. Take an extra minute in the beginning to make sure the communication is clear; this can save you hours of misunderstandings later. Feedback helps strenthen communication. Sometimes there can be discrepancies between what we think we've said and what others think they've heard. After you've told someone something, ask for that person to repeat what you said so you can be certain that you communicated properly: "Just to be sure *I've* explained it clearly, would you repeat what I said?" Likewise, if someone has explained something poorly to you, don't accuse him or her of unclear communication. Instead, say, "I want to be sure I understand you clearly; what you want is . . ."

HOW TO BE A GOOD LISTENER

Telephone, a game many of us played as children, illustrates how messages can be distorted and how careless listening can cause problems. In the game, one person whispers a message to a second person, who whispers it to a third. The message is passed around the circle with everyone listening as carefully as possible. However, the message is almost always distorted by the time it reaches the last person, who says it out loud. If messages can change so drastically when everyone is concentrating on getting them correctly, how much more jumbled can communications get in a busy office where there are countless distractions, interruptions, and people coming and going?

People often listen with their own psychological filters, hearing what they want to, or need to, hear. And yet, many people spend most of their business days listening to others.

HOW DO *YOU* RATE AS A LISTENER?

	ALWAYS	USUALLY	SOMETIMES	NEVER
1. Do you pay close attention when others are talking?	⎯⎯	⎯⎯	⎯⎯	⎯⎯
2. Do you make extended eye contact?	⎯⎯	⎯⎯	⎯⎯	⎯⎯
3. Do you give nonverbal feedback, such as nodding your head, to indicate that you are listening?	⎯⎯	⎯⎯	⎯⎯	⎯⎯
4. Do you take notes when others give you directions and important information?	⎯⎯	⎯⎯	⎯⎯	⎯⎯
5. Do you let others finish talking before you begin?	⎯⎯	⎯⎯	⎯⎯	⎯⎯
6. Do you stick to the subject in conversations rather than go off on tangents?	⎯⎯	⎯⎯	⎯⎯	⎯⎯
7. Do you keep an open mind regarding the points of view of others?	⎯⎯	⎯⎯	⎯⎯	⎯⎯
8. Do you match people's communication styles by speaking in terms they can understand?	⎯⎯	⎯⎯	⎯⎯	⎯⎯
9. Are you interested in what other people have to say?	⎯⎯	⎯⎯	⎯⎯	⎯⎯
10. Are you patient with people who have difficulty expressing themselves?	⎯⎯	⎯⎯	⎯⎯	⎯⎯

YOUR SCORE

Give yourself 4 points for each *always* you checked, 3 points for each *usually,* 2 points for each *sometimes,* and 1 point for each *never.* Add up your points and find yourself below.

35–40: You're a great listener. Keep up the good work!

30–34: Chances are, you listen well to others when it suits you. You could be missing out on important ideas others want to share. To be more sensitive to people more of the time, incorporate the ideas below into your present style of listening.

Below 30: Listen up! You've got a lot of room for improvement. Sharpen your listening skills by cultivating a genuine interest in people. Suspend judgment when others are speaking; wait until they've completed their thoughts to add yours to the conversation. And bear in mind what Zeno of Citium said around 300 B.C.: "The reason why we have two ears and only one mouth is that we may listen the more and talk the less."

1. Keep letters brief and to the point.
2. Use a conversatonal tone.
3. Avoid jargon.
4. Use the active voice. For example, ''We appreciate your contribution,'' not, ''Your contribution is appreciated.''
5. Use form letters for routine business communications.
6. Keep in touch with special people by sending notes or cards for birthdays and special occasions.

Your Action Plan

A. Write down five "I" messages regarding things you've been wanting to communicate to people.
B. Talk to four people today and subtly match their body language and energy levels; observe the results.
C. Next time you give directions to someone else, ask for that person to give you feedback.
D. Practice extended eye contact in the next conversation you have with someone; maintain eye contact for at least two minutes.

_____QUOTE TO CONSIDER_____

"In good conversation, parties don't speak to the words, but to the meanings of each other."

—Ralph Waldo Emerson

19

TIMELY
TECHNOLOGY

OBJECTIVES

When you finish this chapter, you will be able to:

- Use tape recorders more creatively
- Dictate effectively
- Choose from a variety of telephone equipment for your office

Robots whirl down long corridors to pick up and deliver mail. Small business computers perch atop desks and wait for commands. Intelligent typewriters remember phrases and up to nine formats for letters, reports, and forms. Word processors help writers edit almost effortlessly. Printers type up manuscripts while writers lean back and sip coffee. Speaker phones, remote phones, and automatic dialing devices enable you to do something else while on hold, walk around the office and still talk to callers, and program your most frequently called numbers and automatically redial if those numbers are busy. Conference calls eliminate costly business trips, call forwarding follows you wherever you go, and telephone computers make hundreds of marketing calls to potential customers and don't feel rejected if people hang up.

Modern offices virtually hum and buzz and beep with the latest time-saving conveniences. New companies are springing up everywhere and clamoring for your business. Where do you start in all this to update your office equipment? One thing to realize is that modernizing an office is an *evolutionary* process that requires careful research, comparison shopping, and then the addition of a system at a time. But there's an even more elementary step than this, and that's to make sure to get optimum use out of the equipment that you *already* have. One often underrated piece of time-saving equipment is the tape recorder.

TYPES OF TAPE RECORDERS AND SOME CREATIVE USES

1. *Standard portable tape recorders*. These machines are becoming much lighter and more easy to operate. You can use them as *classrooms on wheels* by playing them in your car on the way to work. Have the instructor sitting right next to

you as you play tapes from classes and seminars. Benefit from *spaced repetitious learning*. In one day, we forget about 80 percent of what we've heard. To strengthen your memory, play the tapes periodically over several days or weeks while you are driving, relaxing, or falling asleep at night. Instead of rereading texts and reports, tape the highlights and play them in your spare time.

Keep a permanent record of interviews, important business deals, and meetings with customers or clients. If someone feels uncomfortable about being recorded, wait until right after the meeting, when you can record the important points while they are still fresh in your mind.

Share notes. It's not time-effective to repeat yourself. If you've attended a meeting and others want to know about it, pass your cassette on to them and let them listen on their own time while you get back to work.

Tape letters. For a change of pace, record letters to friends and family. Add to the cassette as ideas come to you. You might want to ask listeners to pass the tape on to others who would be interested in hearing from you.

2. *Telephone answering machines.* In many cases, it's more effective to have your phone answered by a tape recorder than not to have it answered at all—in spite of people's complaints about talking to a machine. Answering machines are more convenient nowadays. *Voice-activated tapes* allow callers to record their entire message without being cut off. If you're at home, some machines allow you to *monitor your calls,* to listen to incoming messages and decide if you want to speak with the caller. You can then save tapes as permanent records of your calls. Some machines allow you to record telephone conversations, but it is illegal to do so without the other person's express permission.

When you are away from home or office, *remote control devices* enable you to call your answering machine for messages.

When making a tape for your answering machine, be sure to ask for the caller's name, phone number, best time for you to return the call, nature of the caller's business, and the date. Then instruct callers to wait for the tone to leave messages. If they speak *before* the tone, that part of the message will be lost.

3. *Speed-controlled recorders.* These recorders allow you to *speed-listen* to any regular audio cassette tape. By adjusting the rate, you can reduce your listening time to less than half the time it would take you to listen on a conventional recorder. The speech *is* speeded up, but some recorders are designed to keep the tape from sounding like frantic chipmunks. With speed listening, there's little time for the mind to wander—a significant asset for people who have to listen to large amounts of material.

4. *Dictating Machines.* Use these valuable recorders to dictate action items, highlight salient points for your secretary to draft into letters and reports, and to capture flashes of insights that you have.

When dictating for someone else to transcribe, use the following guidelines.

Organize you thoughts beforehand. Jot down the points you want covered in your letter or report. When you begin dictating, your thoughts will flow more smoothly.

Stop for think time. If your dictating machine is not voice-activated, stop it when you are thinking so you don't waste your secretary's time listening to blank tape.

Give your secretary the big picture. Prepare your secretary at the beginning of the tape. Communicate approximately how long the tape will be and whether it is a letter, report, or some other kind of business communication.

Spell difficult words, enunciate clearly, and designate punctuation and beginnings of paragraphs.

Erase your mistakes. Don't switch ideas in midsentence without erasing the sentence you already began. Having a rough outline beforehand of your thoughts should help reduce scattered thinking.

Eliminate background noise. As much as possible, dictate in a quiet setting.

TELEPHONE TECHNOLOGY

We've come a long way since Alexander Graham Bell. Modernize your office with the following fascinating equipment.

1. Telephone answering machines take your calls while you're out, or enable you to listen to incoming calls and decide whether or not to answer. Some models are voice-activated.
2. Cordless phones allow you to carry on a conversation while walking about the office or the building.
3. Automatic dialing stores frequently called numbers in its memory. To dial, push one or two code numbers. Automatic redial allows you to redial the last number you called by hitting the redial button. If the number is busy, the unit redials at programmed intervals.
4. Speaker phones enable you to talk to the other party without having to hold the phone to your ear. This frees you to do other things while talking or if you're put on hold.
5. Call-forwarding automatically forwards your incoming calls to the new number you've designated. You never miss a call this way.
6. Call-waiting signals that someone else is trying to reach you when you're on the phone with another party.
7. Conference calls allow you to talk long distance with several parties, thus eliminating time-consuming travel. Check with the conference call operator for details.

Your Action Plan

A. If you don't already have one, buy a tape recorder and begin putting it to use.
B. Research telephone devices and the feasibility of using them in your business.

20

HELP FOR THE ABSENT-MINDED

When you finish this chapter, you will be able to:

- Remember upcoming events and important dates
- Remember where you put things
- Better focus on what you're doing
- Motivate yourself to remember

	OFTEN	SOMETIMES	NEVER

1. Do you forget where you parked your car? _____ _____ _____

2. Do you misplace things? _____ _____ _____

3. Do you forget birthdays, anniversaries, important meetings, appointments, or other special occasions? _____ _____ _____

4. Do you go to the store and return with everything but the item you went to buy? _____ _____ _____

5. Do you have people return your phone calls only to forget why you called them in the first place? _____ _____ _____

6. Do you realize there was something you forgot to say *after* hanging up the phone? _____ _____ _____

7. Do you do one thing while thinking something else? _____ _____ _____

8. Do you lock yourself out of your car? _____ _____ _____

9. Do you leave the house to go somewhere and have to return for something you forgot? _____ _____ _____

10. Do you put things in the wrong places, such as your keys in the refrigerator or the milk in the cupboard? _____ _____ _____

11. Do you lose your train of thought? _____ _____ _____

12. Do you forget to zip zippers, to button buttons, to clamp clamps? _____ _____ _____

13. Do you do something more than once because you forgot that you did it in the first place? _____ _____ _____

14. Do you forget to do things that you intended to do? _____ _____ _____

15. Do you become so absorbed in thought that you lose awareness of your surroundings? _____ _____ _____

Your Score

Give yourself 3 points for each often you checked, 2 points for each sometimes, and 1 point for each never. Add up your score and find yourself below.

Below 16: Congratulations! Your memory is so good, you could give an elephant competition.

16–29: Your memory is pretty good but it could use some shaping up. You may be suffering from scattered thinking due to the pitfalls of a busy life. The following suggestions can help you through annoying periods of distractability.

30–45: You're probably plagued by the "absent-minded professor" syndrome. Nip forgetfulness in the bud before it becomes an ingrained habit. Jot down the best ideas you glean from this chapter and carry the notes with you for reference. Don't misplace your notes!

Being forgetful can be very annoying. It's time-consuming trying to find your car at a crowded airport, or to retrace your steps in an attempt to locate your books, briefcase, hat, or umbrella that you left *somewhere*. And often, being absent-minded is just downright embarrassing! People have reported pouring their breakfast cereal into the cat's dish, popping both contact lenses into the *same* eye, forgetting their boss's name during introductions, and frantically searching for their sunglasses, which everyone else sees perched on top of their heads.

Absent-mindedness is comprised of three kinds of forgetfulness: 1) forgetting where you put things; 2) forgetting upcoming events; 3) forgetting what you're doing at the moment. Such forgetfulness can be brought on by circumstances. For example, you may feel pressured or overwhelmed at work. You can give no particular task your full attention when endeavoring to do several things at once. Scattered thinking is the perfect breeding ground for absent-mindedness. Forgetfulness may also have a nutritional cause: too much caffeine or alcohol, overeating, undereating, or low blood sugar. Or forgetfulness might have started as a result of one of these causes and evolved into lifelong bad habits of inattentiveness, poor concentration, or lack of mental discipline.

The following suggestions are not intended as a replacement for building a good memory, but they can help you over periodic bouts with absent-mindedness. Many of the ideas below have been proposed by reformed forgetters who have found them to be valuable aids to memory.

How to Remember Upcoming Events and Important Dates

1. *Keep a "tickler" file.* Set up a tickler file system as described in Chapter 5. To jog your memory, be sure to look in your tickler file every morning.

George, a manager in a busy company, shares a clever way to use a tickler file. "I'm not a sentimental person by nature, but many people do like to be remembered on their birthdays and on special occasions. One afternoon a year, early in January, I set some time aside and jot down all the birthdays and anniversaries that I want to remember for that year. Then I go out, buy cards for every occasion, sign them, and slip them into their respective folders. This way, I automatically remember special occasions. If I'm on a business trip, my secretary mails the cards."

2. *Carefully organize your day.* A successful military recruiter states that he never has any trouble with absent-mindedness. "We recruiters keep track of everything we need to do each day in a 'scheduling and results' book. When we finish an item, we analyze the information and record the results. Our books are always organized. We're fined fifty-dollars a page for each page that isn't kept up-to-date."

A civilian equivalent of the "scheduling and results" book is a well thought-out planning system and the self-discipline to keep it current. Include in your planning system a tickler file, a to-do list, your short-term and long-term goals in writing, and a monthly calendar-at-a-glance.

3. *Use "can't miss" reminders.* A business consultant recommends that, "When you have an important letter to mail, balance it on the doorknob where you can't possibly overlook it when you leave. By the same token, if you have library books to return, pile them in the doorway so you have to step over them when you go out." And this idea from a self-employed businesswoman: "When I have an important call to make or a meeting to attend that day, I tape a notice to the bathroom mirror so I see it first thing in the morning. Then, of course, I also have it written on my to-do list." And this from a cook: "With a broken timer on my oven and no alarm clock, I have to be careful that things in the oven don't burn. So I carry a tablespoon around with me as a reminder to check the oven every so often. If I'm doing something else, I set the tablespoon in my lap—it's never failed to remind me!"

HOW TO REMEMBER WHERE YOU PUT THINGS

1. *Have a parking place for everything.* Jane, a busy entrepreneur with three businesses, observes that, "Somehow we always take time to look for items that we've lost, but we don't necessarily take time to put them in regular places so we can find them easily. For example, a friend of mine misplaced a fifty dollar bonus check she received. She spent a great deal of time frantically turning the house upside down in search of it. She finally took the trash apart piece by piece and discovered that she had absent-mindedly thrown the check in the rubbish. She could save herself a lot of trouble in the future if she immediately puts all checks she receives into her checkbook so she finds them right away when she goes to the bank. Of course, she'll have to have a parking place for her checkbook, too, so she knows where to find *that* every time."

2. *Make visual associations.* Memory experts Harry Lorayne and Jerry Lucas, in their book *The Memory Book,* suggest a creative way to overcome absent-mindedness. In order to have something register in your mind at the moment you're doing it, form instant associations. One salesman used this strategy when he parked his car in a large, seven-tiered parking garage. "I didn't have paper with me to jot down where I parked so I formed an association. I parked my car on the third level, section A. Three rhymes with tree, so I imagined driving my Automobile up a tall tree and hanging it on the uppermost branch like a Christmas tree ornament. I associated the letter 'A' with Automobile. Tree-A. I formed the association much faster than I can explain it—and it worked!"

3. *Connect items to remember them.* To remember items when you're out in public or while in transit, consider some of the solutions proposed by previously absent-minded people: "Since I always remember my purse, I hook my umbrella through my purse handle so I remember them both. If I'm carrying report folders with me, I set them on *top* of my purse." "I used to forget my hat. Now when I'm in restaurants, I place my hat on the seat next to me, *on the outside,* so I slide into it when I'm leaving."

HOW TO KEEP YOUR MIND ON WHAT YOU'RE DOING

1. *Don't defend absent-mindedness.* One of the most common defenses for being forgetful is: "Well, Albert Einstein was absent-minded and *he* was a genius!" People who use this excuse may be implying that their thoughts are too lofty to pay attention to the mundane world about them. But sometimes it takes as much genius to keep your mind on what you're doing and to succeed in the challenging world of today as it does to escape into inattentiveness for whatever the reason.

2. *Make a conscious commitment to be more aware.* If it's awesome to think that you'll have to remember everything from now on for the rest of your life, simply vow to be more attentive for the duration of a meeting or until the end of a particular conversation. Then extend your periods of concentration to a whole morning at work, then to an entire day. This helps focus your thinking, and the more you remember, the more faith you'll have in your memory. Practice this exercise now by giving your complete attention to the rest of the information in this chapter.

3. *Live in the present.* Think about what's happening now, rather than being worried about what you're going to do or say, or about what you've already done or said. John, a technical writer, learned this the hard way. He'd been writing a chapter for a book on his word processor. His mind wasn't really on his work. He was thinking about an important meeting he was going to have with his agent later on that day. When John stopped for lunch, he flipped off the light switch to save energy. What he neglected to save was the last four pages of his text. They were erased from the memory of his computer when he switched off the power. Now John keeps his mind on what he's doing. He is also in the habit of putting a piece of tape over the light switch as a safeguard whenever he turns on his computer.

4. *Make checklists.* Before you have to be somewhere, make a list of everything you want to do before you leave. Include on your list everything you need to take with you. Build a time cushion into your travel time. This way, you don't rush around at the last minute trying to remember everything.

5. *Record what you want to remember.* Carry a pad of paper or a small tape recorder with you for all those odds and ends you want to remember throughout the day. If a great idea comes to you during the night, jot down or record just the key phrases to jog your memory in the morning.

6. *Talk to yourself.* Have you ever gone out on a cold day and discovered a dead battery in your car because you left the lights on? To prevent this in the future, you might talk to yourself the next time you turn on your lights earlier than usual: "I'm turning on the headlights. . . . I don't normally turn them on this early in the afternoon, but it's so overcast, it's a good idea to turn them on. . . . I'll remember to turn them off when I get to my destination. If I forget, I could run down the battery and that could cause a lot of problems. . . . Looks like most of the other cars have their lights on, too. . . ." This may sound like an exaggerated way to remember, but it's unbeatable in helping you keep your mind on what you're doing at the moment.

7. *Motivate yourself to remember.* If someone fined you $50 every time you forgot something, could you remember? Most likely you could. If this is the case, your absent-mindedness could be due to a lack of motivation to remember. Take a few minutes now and think back on all the aggravation and embarrassment you've

caused yourself by being absent-minded. Weigh this against the effort of following the suggestions in this chapter. Then make the commitment to be more aware.

Realize that your memory is already excellent. Every day, you remember thousands of things. With a little effort and the ideas in this chapter, you can reduce those periods of absent-mindedness. You'll begin to agree with memory expert James D. Weinland, who states in his book *How to Improve Your Memory* that, "The amazing thing is not that we forget but that we remember so much."

Your Action Plan

Make the commitment to be more aware in your life. If absent-mindedness has been a problem for you, put the ideas in this chapter into practice.

_____ QUOTE TO CONSIDER:_____

"Memory is the power to gather roses in winter."
—Dr. Ewen Cameron

21

HOW TO REDUCE STRESS WITH GOOD TIME MANAGEMENT

OBJECTIVES

When you finish this chapter, you will be able to:

- Better pace yourself to avoid stress
- Salvage hectic days
- Constructively channel your energy if you're a workaholic
- Visualize a perfect day to more easily identify and develop positive time-management habits

SAY "OLÉ" TO PRESSURE

A woman once shared with me the story of a hike she took. "I was in the country walking across a large meadow. There were three cows standing over by the fence. As I continued to walk, I noticed that one of the 'cows' was watching me very intently, pawing the ground, and snorting. I realized to my horror that it was a bull getting ready to charge. My whole body changed in a split second. My stomach had that sinking feeling, my breathing became very shallow, my hands turned to ice, and my blood pressure must have shot through the roof. I was ready to do one terrific sprint to a stand of trees at the edge of the meadow. With that half-ton bull after me, I could have done the one-minute mile easily!"

Should the bull have charged (which fortunately it did not), the stress reaction had prepared this woman for fight or flight. Similar stress reactions help athletes excel at sports during competitions. And it helps us through business crises and tight deadlines. When faced with threatening or challenging situations, stress revs us up and sees us through.

The danger arises if we make a habit of functioning at stress levels, which leads to chronic tension. We can become so accustomed to stress that we lose our awareness of it. In this case, some people seek even higher levels of stress to fill their need for excitement; they may actually create situations in which they have tight deadlines, angry bosses, frantic finishes, and other crises. The human body is designed to return to normal after a stressful situation. However, if tension is the rule rather than the exception, it may be increasingly more difficult to stabilize the body's functions; blood pressure may remain dangerously high, indigestion may become acute, and it may be more difficult to relax.

Dancers, actors, and public speakers sometimes report a feeling of "letdown" when their performances are over. Writers may experience mild depressions when they finally complete their books. Business people can have similar reactions when the rush is over, the quarterly report is turned in at last, the deal is finalized, and the fires are extinguished.

The remedy for "letdown" is to realize that this feeling is simply your body returning to normal after a period of stress. Guard against the mistake many people make of diving immediately into more projects to keep the momentum going. Use lulls to regroup your thoughts, set new goals, and celebrate your accomplishments. Robert G., a novelist, celebrated completing a novel by starting to write a second book the same hour he finished the first. "Then I realized what I was doing. I thought, good heavens! You just wrote a *book!* Go out and have some fun!"

WHAT TO DO WHEN IT'S BEEN ONE OF *THOSE* DAYS!

Occasionally, you may have one of *those* days when nothing seems to go right. It can start with your being late to the office. Already behind in your work, your problems are compounded when your clients are unprepared for their appointments. A staff meeting starts late. The office doesn't have the supplies you need and you spend your lunch hour scurrying all over town trying to find some. Customers tie you up with complaints and you miss your afternoon break. It's 3:30 and you still have twelve items left on your to-do list. You have a 5 P.M. deadline on a project and your boss just asked you for a ride to the airport because the company car is in the shop. You're desperate. How can good time management help you salvage hectic, horrible days like this one?

Take five. Stop for a moment to collect your thoughts. More than ever, you need to be relaxed and clear-thinking. Clean a space off your desk to make it seem less cluttered. Put away everything you can.

Revise what needs to be done. Some of the items on your to-do list clearly *must go.* Imagine that you're a battlefield doctor who is overwhelmed with wounded and because of your limited time and resources, you must decide which soldiers you can save and which you must let die. Determine which of the day's activities you can rescue and which you must let expire. Some, with a little attention, can be kept alive until later when you have more time. For example, if you've promised someone a report, call that person with a progress report; let him or her know what you've accomplished so far and when you'll have the rest of the information. This way, the other person doesn't feel abandoned by you, and you've bought yourself some more time.

Renegotiate deadlines. Your deadline may not be written in stone. Explain the situation to the people involved and ask if you can push back the deadline. If you're in danger of missing a deadline, let others know as soon as possible to minimize the inconvenience to them. If customers are expecting their orders, make (or delegate) a quick phone call to them to let them know the status of those orders; don't just let things "slip," or it could harm customer relations.

Procrastinate selectively. Postpone all the trivia you possibly can for another day. Rather than tiring yourself out by working two hours late to finish everything, consider working just twenty-five minutes extra each day for the rest of the week.

Find alternative plans. If your boss has asked for a favor such as a ride to the airport, explain about your time crunch. Maybe you can come up with another solution together: Your boss might take a taxi to the airport or ask someone else for a ride.

Send representatives to routine meetings. Have your secretary or administrative assistant attend routine meetings in your place until the crisis has passed. Or ask co-workers to take notes for you.

Reset your priorities. Communicate your problem to your boss and ask for help resetting the day's priorities. Request more lead time on future projects.

Improve your concentration. Avoid impulse chores such as making unnecessary phone calls. Cut off your escapes. Put away distracting material such as magazines. Hang a sign on your door: "Fire fighting until ____P.M. Do not enter unless it's an emergency!"

Shorten breaks. Shorten your lunch hour and breaks, but don't skip them. You need to maintain your energy. You might want to divide a fifteen-minute break into one five-minute break every hour; during this time, do some stretching exercises, some deep breathing, and pull your thoughts together.

Use temporary help. Keep a list on hand of temporary help agencies who can send last-minute reinforcements to help you handle crises.

Cash in on favors. If people owe you favors, now's the time to collect. Be very sure, however, that this is a genuine emergency and that you aren't just "crying wolf." Don't expect others to help you if crisis situations are regular occurrences for you. And be willing to reciprocate when others need help.

Gain perspective. When one of *those* days is finally over, reevaluate what went wrong and why things piled up. Learn from the situation and find ways to prevent problems in the future. Do you need more lead time on projects? Could you be more assertive? Do you need to redefine your goals? Can you delegate more? Would it help you to establish checkpoints along the way for a lengthy project to make sure things are going according to plan?

Ask yourself how this one day is going to fit in with the rest of your life. Remember, for each bad day, there are many more that run smoothly.

WORKAHOLICS I'VE MET:

Are quick-witted

Are fast thinkers

Love to work hard

Live for their work

Have very high standards

Cannot tolerate inactivity

Tend to be high-energy people

Have a strong need to achieve

Are quickly bored by routine work

Thrive on competition and challenge

Try to do more than one thing at a time

Try to go in too many directions at once

Cannot easily turn off work at the end of the day

Have trouble balancing their business and personal lives

Take their stress home at the end of the day

Feel guilty if they slow down and relax

Take on more work than they can handle

May get behind in their work

Rank high on stress charts

Overextend themselves

Often take work home

WHAT ABOUT *YOU?*

It's commendable to be a high achiever. However, workaholics have to guard against making work their entire lives. If you suffer from workaholism, kick the habit and learn to channel your powerful mental energies by doing the following:

1. Clarify your valued objectives in life.
2. Develop a satisfying personal life that balances your professional life.
3. Have clearcut goals so you don't go off on tangents.
4. Finish projects fully before starting new projects.
5. Limit the number of projects you take on at any one time.
6. Handle stress by following the suggestions in this chapter. Laugh more often. Have fun.

YOUR IDEAL DAY

Positive mental pictures can help you develop strong, effective time-management habits. Treat your subconscious mind to a visit to an imaginary ideal day. Fill in the details to fit your particular situation. As the day begins . . .

You wake up alert, refreshed, and in a positive state of mind. After eating a substantial, nourishing breakfast, you allow a time cushion for getting to work in case of traffic jams or unexpected delays. As you commute to the office, you listen to music or educational tapes. If you're a passenger, you read or finish planning your day.

When you get to work, your day is already planned. Using the personal time log you've been keeping, you've been able to estimate how much work you can accomplish during the day. With this guideline, you've outlined a successful day for yourself. Your to-do list is realistic; you'll add items if you finish early. Your office is well organized, and your desk is clean.

You make the rounds quickly. You check with people to see if they have any pressing questions for you, and you inform them that you'll be unavailable for the next hour. You meet briefly with your boss if you have one, and discuss what needs to be done during the day.

You hang out your quiet hour sign. This protected time is precious, because in this hour, you'll accomplish what it used to take you two or three hours to do. During your earlier planning time, you identified your elephant for the day, the most important high-payoff project on which to work during your morning peak time. If you wait until later, something unexpected might arise and prevent you from hunting your elephant. Today, it's a particularly large elephant; you have to wait for someone to bring you some information later, so you work on the project for half an hour. After that, you work on another major project until your quiet hour is up. In these two half-hour units, you've accomplished a great deal of work.

You handle interruptions assertively. You've asked people to group their questions rather than trail into your office with one question at a time. When someone does come in, you inquire how much time this person needs, and you limit his or her visit. If he or she needs more time, you arrange a later appointment.

You've further reduced interruptions by informing callers about the best times to reach you. Your assistant is holding all low-priority items until you meet with him or her later that day. Messages are put in a special place you've designated; this reduces interruptions and you're free to check the grouped messages when you have time.

You discipline yourself not to interrupt others, and you know when the best time is to reach them. You group your phone calls, jot down what you want to say beforehand, and use good telephone equipment. A speaker phone allows you to work on something else while you're waiting for them to answer. An autodialer redials the number if it's busy. If you're put on hold, you have work and reading material handy. When you have finished with the phone call, you complete the necessary information in your telephone log.

Relaxed and on target, you enjoy your break. During your break, you reflect on how well the morning has been going. You're careful not to let your break run overtime. After your break, you tie up loose ends, check your messages, return phone calls, and meet with staff people who've made appointments to discuss more lengthy matters. Before you go to lunch, you take ten minutes to straighten up your office.

You eat a light, nutritious lunch. To keep your energy high, you go for a short walk after lunch, and return in a relaxed, positive frame of mind.

To reduce paperwork, you prioritize your mail. When you open your mail, dump or delegate as much as possible. Put material that isn't time-critical into your briefcase to read later. Only about one-fourth of the mail now demands your careful attention. You work on it until your meeting.

The meeting goes well. During a prior meeting, you asked that time limits be set on meetings and that agendas be distributed beforehand. Consequently, everyone has thought about the items earlier and the meeting is on target. All the items are handled, and everyone is satisfied that the time has been well spent.

You handle paperwork quickly. Back at your desk, you work to natural stopping places, and to completion. A series of wins throughout the day has kept your energy high. At break time, you find a hideaway and meditate. After ten minutes, you return feeling refreshed and clear-headed.

Your afternoon appointments go well. Your first client is prepared with questions and information, so no time is wasted during the meeting. Your second appointment is fifteen minutes late, and during this time you whittle away at your "delay" pile of reading.

You've penciled yourself in on your daily calendar, and now spend a few minutes reading important journals. You scan the contents and read the most important articles first. You tear out the articles you want to keep, and put them into a topic file of related material rather than save the entire magazine.

Before you go home, you plan tomorrow. Your to-do list was realistic and you finished it. You jotted down two items that were not originally on your list, and you realize that you've accomplished more than you had intended to. You evaluate the day and plan the next, then spend five minutes again straightening up your office. On the way home, you listen to music tapes and congratulate yourself on your productive day.

Home time is quality time. Because you've identified your personal goals, you spend quality time with friends and family. In addition, you pursue other interests such as exercise and hobbies.

It's been a great day. You've replaced your old, ineffective time-management habits with more practical practices. You have a greater understanding of how you use your time. You set goals and priorities. Your desk and files are organized. You handle paperwork quickly, deal assertively with those who interrupt you, delegate when possible, and start and finish projects on time. Through better time management, you are building a richer life for yourself—a *real* achievement!

ON TOP OF THE WORLD
WITH GOOD TIME MANAGEMENT

APPENDIX

I

BE YOUR OWN TIME-MANAGEMENT CONSULTANT

As a review, list all the ways to:

1. Reduce time spent on paperwork
2. Spend less time on the phone
3. Reduce interruptions
4. Use PERT flow charts
5. Delegate more effectively
6. Become more decisive
7. Overcome procrastination
8. Use the 80/20 principle
9. Increase time spent on high-payoff items
10. Reduce time spent on low-priority items
11. Have dynamic meetings
12. Save time reading, writing, and sleeping
13. Reduce time spent on meetings
14. Overcome absent-mindedness
15. Schedule your day for maximum effectiveness
16. Use your workspace as your closest ally in your war against wasting time
17. Maintain a clean, organized desk
18. Work faster
19. Do less
20. Control bad time-management habits
21. Write an effective to-do list
22. Reduce stress with good time management
23. Make the most of travel and commute time
24. Communicate effectively with others

APPENDIX
II

week of: _____

goals: (a) _____
(b) _____
(c) _____

action items:

payoff · hi p.o. = 1; med p.o. = 2; lo p.o. = 3
priority · hi pri = A; med pri = B; lo pri = C

	p.o.	pri	
1			
2			
3			
4			
5			
6			
7			
8			
9			
10			
11			
12			
13			
14			
15			
16			
17			
18			
19			
20			
21			
22			
23			
24			
25			

successful week of:

	monday	tuesday	wednesday	thursday
7				
9				
11				
noon				
1				
3				
5				
7				

	friday	saturday	sunday	activities to be scheduled:
7				
9				
11				
noon				
1				
3				
5				
7				

c

day: _____

goals: (a) _____
         (b) _____
         (c) _____

action items:

payoff - hi p.o. = 1; med p.o. = 2; lo p.o. = 3
priority - hi pri = A; med pri = B; lo pri = C

p.o.	pri	

phone calls:

action flow

7:30	
8:00	
8:30	
9:00	
9:30	
10:00	
10:30	
11:00	
11:30	
noon	
12:30	
1:00	
1:30	
2:00	
2:30	
3:00	
3:30	
4:00	
4:30	
5:00	
5:30	
6:00	
6:30	
7:00	

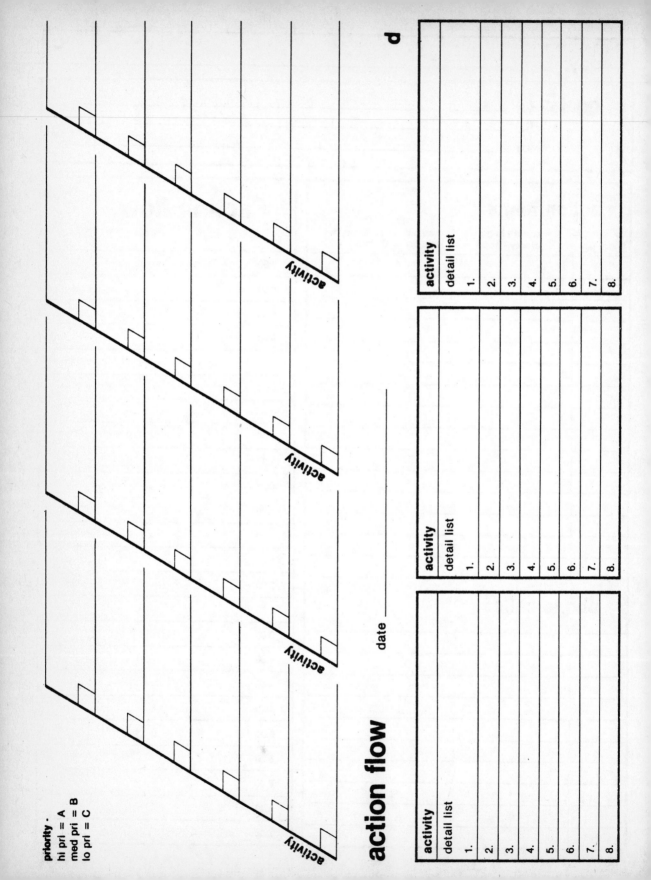

action flow

priority -
hi pri = A
med pri = B
lo pri = C

activity

activity

activity

activity

date _____

activity

detail list
1.
2.
3.
4.
5.
6.
7.
8.

activity

detail list
1.
2.
3.
4.
5.
6.
7.
8.

activity

detail list
1.
2.
3.
4.
5.
6.
7.
8.

time log

time	time invested est.	act.	activity	% effectiveness · how can I handle it more effectively next time?

APPENDIX
III

IN CASE OF EMERGENCY—READ THIS SECTION. . . .

APPOINTMENTS

Call ahead to make sure people are on schedule if you have an appointment with them; if they cancel appointments with you, have alternative plans for that time slot.

BAD TIME-MANAGEMENT HABITS

Write down the habit you want to change, write your goal in finished form, make results measurable, list problems you create with the habit, list benefits of changing the habit, start changing the habit at the next available opportunity, exaggerate the positive traits you want to develop, use affirmations, visually rehearse your new behavior, reward yourself.

COMMUNICATING

Use "I" messages, respect people's peak times, prepare for other's habits, praise others, align priorities, communicate without making others defensive, respect communication styles, encourage feedback, make extended eye contact, keep an open mind regarding different points of view, be genuinely interested in others, share time-management strategies.

COMMUTING

Organize commuting time, share rides, rehearse speeches and interviews, practice presentations, dictate, listen to tapes, map the best routes, use frontage roads for detours, use flextime at work, live close to your job or near major transportation routes, stay relaxed.

DECISION-MAKING

Set goals, clarify your values, use both primary and supplementary sources when you research, avoid paralysis of analysis, use the Ben Franklin strategy, ask the world's greatest authority, decide something!

DELEGATING

Clarify expectations, divide projects into segments and set deadlines for each, designate degree of authority, allow time cushions, set up project checkpoints along the way, evaluate the risk factor, delay criticism, be liberal with praise, avoid upward delegation, ask employees to come to you with solutions instead of problems.

INTERRUPTIONS

Hide out, handle appointments over the phone when possible, arrange regular staff meetings to deal with company business, ask employees to group their questions for you, communicate honestly, be assertive, implement a quiet hour, meet people at *their* desks, reduce personal contact while working, develop secret signals with co-workers to rescue you if you're being interrupted. Stand up to interruptions.

LOW-PAYOFF ACTIVITIES

Delegate them, trade them with someone else, systematize them, ignore them, pay someone else to do them, group them and do them all at once.

MEETINGS

Find alternatives to having meetings, send staff memos instead, send representatives to meetings instead of having everyone attend, hold conference calls, always have an agenda, set short time limits on meetings, start on time, end on time, have "stand-up" meetings, change the style of presentation, use visual aids, get people involved, brainstorm, speak up if meetings get off target.

PAPERWORK

Begin a dump drawer, develop a parking system for everything that comes into your office, when in doubt—throw it out, plan a trivia session, dump it, delay it, delegate it, do it, telephone whenever possible, agree on what to file—don't keep everything, handle each piece of paper once, don't ask for it, answer correspondence briefly, use postcards when possible, streamline your files, set time limits on keeping information, use topic files, make a tickler file, give it away, use it, throw it away, sell it.

PERFECTIONISM

Recognize that below average to a perfectionist is often perfectly acceptable to others, let your purpose for doing a job determine how much time you spend doing it, recognize the point of diminishing returns, get the big picture, learn from your mistakes.

PHYSICAL TENSION

Exercise, eat right.

POORLY PLANNED TO-DO LISTS

Write a to-do list every day, schedule realistically, be aware of limitations on your time frame, allow time cushions, delegate when possible, review your list throughout the day, do at least one major item every day, stay focused on your elephants, minimize ant stomping, be willing to revise your plans if unexpected things come up, group related activities, always write your plans in pencil.

PROCRASTINATION

Put your goal in writing, build motivation, want to do the things you have to do, list benefits you'll enjoy for having achieved your goal, list consequences of not attaining your goal, use the salami method, GOYA, work on the project "just ten minutes," make it a game to finish, cut off your escapes, stay in the vicinity, work to natural stopping places, use the buddy system, start—no matter what, *start!*

PSYCHOLOGICAL TENSION

Speed-sleep, eat right, meditate, keep your perspective.

READING

Speed-read, preview, pace yourself as you read, reduce subvocalization, target-read, apply what you've learned, know where the important information is, read selectively, prioritize reading, limit subscriptions, make appointments to read, swap reading, get good value out of reading time, read in bites, get off mailing lists.

TAKING NOTES AND MESSAGES

Speed-write.

TELEPHONE INTERRUPTIONS

Use the rotation system, don't ask open-ended questions, tell callers you're busy, suggest a better time for people to call, let others know when you're available to receive calls, avoid telephone tag, use a good call-back system, delegate your trivial return calls, set a time limit on your phone calls.

TRAFFIC JAMS

Play tapes, carry reading material with you, dictate, do some creative thinking.

TRAVELING

Decide if the trip is necessary, use a good travel agent, keep a checklist of what to pack, have alternative travel plans, travel lightly, prepare luggage for easy handling, carry important numbers with you, research temperatures in cities you'll be visiting, allow for unexpected delays, carry snacks with you, never assume anything, set up a portable office in your briefcase.

WAITING IN LINE

Carry reading material with you, don't be resentful (it won't make the line move any faster), be patient.

INDEX